THE SAN MARCOS 10

THE SAN MARCOS 10
AN ANTIWAR PROTEST IN TEXAS

E.R. BILLS

Introduction by Joe R. Lansdale

THE
History
PRESS

Published by The History Press
Charleston, SC
www.historypress.com

Copyright © 2019 by E.R. Bills
All rights reserved

Front and back cover images courtesy of the University Archives, Texas State University.

First published 2019

Manufactured in the United States

ISBN 9781467141277

Library of Congress Control Number: 2019945055

I would like to be able to love my country and still love justice.

—Albert Camus

This attempt to tell the story of the San Marcos 10 is dedicated to the namesake participants and all the other contrarians along the way.

CONTENTS

Acknowledgements   11
Introduction, by Joe R. Lansdale   13

1. San Marcos 10   15
2. The Latest Hula Hoop   21
3. First Texas State University "Mobe"   28
4. First Texas State University Mobe's Foes   34
5. Anti-Protest Protest   39
6. Sick Society   66
7. McCrocklin Debacle   78
8. Dissecting Time   95
9. Reinstatement   105
10. Dean-Splaining   125
11. Illusions   135
12. Awful Brood of Prejudice   148
13. Martine's Scam   156
14. Civil Obedience   168
15. Postscript   173

Notes   177
Bibliography   189
Index   197
About the Author   207

ACKNOWLEDGEMENTS

I received an excellent education at (Southwest) Texas State University. I had top-flight professors and instructors whose erudition and wit I still only aspire to match, much less demonstrate my worthiness of. I was also surrounded by talented friends and classmates (and the occasional antagonist), who challenged and inspired me more than they know. Below is a list of some of these exceptional folks. I am indebted to them all.

Roland Alvarado, Susan Ayala, Paul Beck, Rebecca Bell-Metereau, Lisa Jones Bock, Scot Courtney, Quita Culpepper, Patricia A. Deduck, John Demarree, Jody Dodd, Dane Fayle, Jim Garber, David Hiott, Debbie Hiott, R.B. Jager, Jerry Keir, Edgar Laird, Vincent Luizzi, Donald Olson, Norman Peterson, Paula Renfro, David Rice, Gary Rice, Scott Ritter, Reggie Rivers, David Robledo, Rachel Sanborn, Rene Sauceda, Darryl Smyers, Todd Snider, Theron Stimmel, Dale Stockstill, Jerome Supple, Brian H. Thornton, Mark Todd, Evelyn Tolbert, Bobby Wellington, Miles Wilson and many others.

INTRODUCTION

Civil disobedience has a long history. Among prominent activists who have used it as a way to object to something they felt was wrong, or just plain unfair, are Henry David Thoreau, Gandhi, Martin Luther King, Rosa Parks, Susan B. Anthony and Muhammad Ali. We can add the San Marcos 10 of Southwest Texas State University (now known as Texas State University) to that list.

The 10 were among a large number of Americans who had come to believe the war in Vietnam was wrong. I was also among those who felt that way, and I still do. It's interesting to note that the 10, and those like them, were demonized at the time, but history has since proven that their objections to that war were well-advised. Vietnam was once touted as a key piece of the Domino Theory, which was the idea that, like dominoes that are stacked and pushed, the fall of one country to communism would lead to the fall of others into the maw of communism. Vietnam itself wasn't, in actuality, so much a precariously stacked domino as it was a straw man. It was presented as an absolute necessity for the maintenance of world stability, but in reality, it was an excuse to pursue foreign resources, an endeavor that led to the useless deaths of approximately fifty-four thousand American soldiers.

Much of the support for the war came from those who had lived through World War II, a war that was universally considered to be, warts and all, a necessary war. And it was. There are reasons to fight in wars, but they should be rare in their necessity. Vietnam was false from the beginning, and it was certainly false from the time of the Gulf of Tonkin incident, when American destroyers were supposedly attacked by the communist government of Vietnam. This event proved to be not only a suspicious claim but also a fraudulent one that was ultimately used to escalate the United States' presence in Vietnam and to pursue a full-scale war.

E.R. Bills has sliced and diced with precision the antiwar protestors who were labeled as the San Marcos 10. They were part of a larger number of demonstrators who voiced their disagreement with U.S. policy in Southeast Asia the day after the first news reports of the infamous My Lai Massacre were released. The butchering of unarmed and non-threatening South Vietnamese was a kind of knee-jerk response from a group of frustrated and demoralized American soldiers who were looking for vengeance. Unarmed civilians, including women, children and the elderly, were slaughtered in an act equal to those of the Nazis during World War II, but this time, the killers were none other than members of the United States military.

In many ways, the My Lai Massacre was the last straw for the Vietnam War, at least as far as blind support went. However, the war limped along for a few more years, growing more unpopular as time went on, until it finally ended in 1973 in what was called "peace with honor." The American military abandoned the war in a less than honorable way, allowing Vietnam to eventually become not only a United States global trade partner but also a tourist destination, containing Vietnam War sites among its attractions. Ironically, capitalism drives Vietnam's economy more than the much-feared falling domino of communism ever did, and we help them pay for it.

As for the San Marcos 10 protest, the dean of students, Floyd Martine, along with an entourage of redneck reactionists in tow, showed up to demand their vigil end. Martine threatened the participants with dismissal from the university, in spite of their demonstration being peaceful. Most of the anti-Vietnam objectors dispersed, but ten of them remained. This is their story and the story of the history that surrounded them, the history they helped shape.

Joe R. Lansdale

1

SAN MARCOS 10

I didn't get my ideas from Mao, Lenin, or Ho.
I got my ideas from the Lone Ranger.
—Jerry Rubin, American antiwar activist and 1960s counterculture icon

When Kenny Rogers and the New Edition rolled through the San Marcos area in 1968, Rogers, a Houston native, had just landed his first Top 10 hit on the *Billboard Hot 100* chart with "Just Dropped In (To See What Condition My Condition Was In)." A catchy nod to psychedelic drug use in the 1960s, the song peaked at number five and would go on to loom large in a bowling alley dream sequence in *The Big Lebowski* thirty years later.[1] But, in 1968, the 1960s still hadn't gained much of a foothold at Southwest Texas State College (now known as Texas State University), so the Student Center gave away over 1,400 tickets for the on-campus show, and most of them probably went unused.

When Rogers and the New Edition toured the country a year later, however, they were singing a different tune. It was called "Ruby, Don't Take Your Love to Town," and it climbed to number six in the *Billboard Hot 100*. The song was about a paralyzed American soldier confined to a bed or wheelchair—a product of that "crazy Asian war"—who watched helplessly as his young wife painted her face and went out looking for what he assumed was extramarital companionship. If Rogers and the New Edition had made a stop in the San Marcos area that year, the show probably would have sold out. San Marcos and Texas State were still conservative backwaters when compared to other parts of the country, but by the end of 1969, that would begin to change.

At approximately 10:00 a.m. on Thursday, November 13, 1969, a group of Texas State students staged an antiwar demonstration in front of the *Fighting Stallions* statue[2] on the west end of the university Quad. The demonstration itself was part of a nationwide event coordinated by the New Mobilization Committee to End the War in Vietnam (New Mobe). The original Mobilization Committee to End the War in Vietnam (MOBE) had focused on larger, single-city protests, staged mostly in the Northeast. The New Mobe, founded at a conference held at Case Western Reserve University in July 1969, promoted multiple protests across the nation.

Working with the Vietnam Moratorium Committee (VMC) and the Student Mobilization Committee (SMC), the New Mobe planned the Moratorium to End the War in Vietnam, which consisted of demonstrations for three successive months in 1969. The first event was scheduled for October, the second for November and the third, if necessary, was discussed for December.

The scene at the foot of the *Fighting Stallions* statue on November 13 was quiet and somber, as news of the My Lai Massacre had just been released the day before.[3] The protesters sat cross-legged and resolute. Some wore black arm bands to mourn the U.S. war dead, and others held placards. One of the signs said, "Vietnam Is an Edsel." Another noted, "44,000 U.S. Dead, for What?" The onlooking crowd was antagonistic and mostly male. Described as cowboys (or more colloquially as "shit-kickers") and "jocks," they initially kept their distance, and many of them stood with their hands in their pockets. The sitting demonstrators remained composed.

Later in the day, a March Against Death began in Washington, D.C. An estimated forty-five thousand participants, each holding a sign bearing the name of a dead U.S. soldier or a razed Vietnamese village, walked from the Arlington National Cemetery to the White House, calling out the name of their soldier or village as they passed. Over the coming weekend, more than 250,000 people marched in Washington, D.C. But on that sunny, mid-November morning in San Marcos, fewer than 50 protesters sat silently around the *Fighting Stallions* statue. They kept to themselves and remained on the grass, careful not to block pedestrian traffic or cause a disturbance.

At around 10:35 a.m., a university official showed up with a female public relations representative at his side. As he approached the demonstrators, the hostile, mostly male onlookers transmogrified into the official's entourage as he issued the following ultimatum:

Ladies and gentlemen. May I have your attention please? I am Floyd Martine, dean of students. In the judgment of the university administration, this assembly is a violation of established university policies as set forth in the student handbook. I hereby direct you to leave this area within three minutes. Any student remaining beyond that time will be suspended from school until the fall of 1970.

The "established university policies set forth in the student handbook" concerned when and where protests could be staged on campus. The designated location was at the other end of the Quad in front of the Old Main administration building. The designated time slots for "Student Expressions" were between 12:00 and 1:00 p.m. and 5:00 and 7:00 p.m.

Martine repeated his statement, gave the group three minutes to clear out and left. As campus security officers began cordoning off the area the demonstrators occupied, most of their number dispersed, but a handful remained. In the meantime, the crowd of cowboys and jocks on the other

The beginning of the November 13, 1969 Vietnam Moratorium sit-in at Texas State University. *Courtesy of the University Archives, Texas State University.*

side of the rope had increased, their numbers bolstered by a vocal "Love It or Leave It" contingent. They taunted and threatened the remaining antiwar protesters and became very loud. A German instructor named Allan Black subsequently stepped under the rope and joined the antiwar group, because he was concerned with how they were being treated.

When Martine returned, he found eleven demonstrators and Mr. Black stationed at or near the base of the *Fighting Stallions*. Amidst jeers of, "Your three minutes are up," and, "Let's drag 'em off," Martine told the group that they were "through at the university" and began taking their names. The public relations representative, Pat Murdock, recorded the exchange.[4] One protester, Adam C. Ravelo, was not enrolled at the college and was ordered to leave by the campus police. He did so voluntarily. The remaining students would later come to be known as the San Marcos 10. They were: twenty-seven-year-old Vietnam veteran David Bayless of Aransas Pass; nineteen-year-old Annie Burleson of Houston; twenty-three-year-old Paul Cates of San Antonio; nineteen-year-old Al Henson of Pasadena; twenty-three-year-old Michael Holman of Austin; twenty-seven-year-old David O. McConchie of Aransas Pass; twenty-four-year-old former soldier Murray Rosenwasser of Lockhart; twenty-one-year-old Joe Saranello of Brooklyn, New York; twenty-year-old Sallie Ann Satagaj of San Antonio; and eighteen-year-old Frances Vykoukal of Sealy. They were all suspended from Texas State on the spot. No action was taken against Mr. Black.

In recent interviews, members of the group recalled the moment:

"It was truly bizarre," Rosenwasser said. "A guy from my hometown was actually one of the guys holding the rope they used to cordon us off."

"The crowd was screaming at us," remembered Satagaj. "'Love it or Leave it!' 'Let's string 'em up!' All kinds of ugly things, and that's why Allan Black came and sat with us."

"I was sitting on the grass, quietly, with my back against the base of the statue, while the onlookers were shouting and trying to intimidate us," said Henson. "And Martine comes out and says they're gonna kick us out of school? I thought, 'What the hell?' To heck with them. They can't do that."

"We had a right to be there," Holman maintained. "We were peacefully demonstrating, and the other side was screaming and yelling. Any disturbance that occurred was caused by the 'kickers.'"

"Martine came out there and tried to treat us like children," Bayless recalled. "It was ridiculous. McConchie already had a kid, and I was just

Onlookers begin to congregate in front of the antiwar protesters at Texas State on November 13, 1969. *Courtesy of the University Archives, Texas State University.*

back from the war. We weren't children. We were very serious. We were hand-in-hand and heart-to-heart. It was a full feeling. We were doing what had to be done."

"I felt very strongly that the war had gone on too long and that it was essentially wrong," said Cates, who had served as a Texas State student senator for two years. "I just wanted to express myself in the demonstration, and I was very much aware that we would be in trouble."

The San Marcos 10 were not alone, even in Texas. On November 13, a group of 150 to 200 antiwar demonstrators up the road at the University of Texas in Austin actually heckled ROTC cadets, chanting, "Peace now, peace now," and, "oink, oink, oink, oink," to the march cadence. Protesters at Southern Methodist University in Dallas constructed a mock graveyard, delivered speeches and read a list of the 2,200 Texans who had been killed in Vietnam. Elsewhere in the city, the Dallas Independent School District sent home 20 high school students for wearing black armbands. In Beaumont, demonstrators at Lamar Tech (now Lamar University) sponsored an open-air teach-in (which included 5 university instructors). In Lamar, 4 students were also arrested for circulating antiwar materials at a local high school. In El Paso, demonstrators carrying white crosses marched from the University of Texas at El Paso's campus to the U.S. Federal Building, where approximately 150 young people held a peaceful moratorium ceremony. In Waco, 100 students attended an antiwar rally in Cameron Park. At Tarleton State University, protesters held a symposium and a prayer service. A few days earlier, demonstrators at Rice University barricaded the Placement Office to block Central Intelligence Agency (CIA) recruiters from conducting interviews.[5]

The San Marcos 10 hadn't created mock graveyards, marched through the campus, barricaded buildings, derided their ROTC classmates, read lists of the war dead or even given speeches. They had simply taken part in a silent vigil.

2

THE LATEST HULA HOOP

*Most students—in England and America—are not interested in study or learning.
They are just interested in playing the particular game they have been taught to
play by their parental, religious, national, or ideological affiliations. Thought is
painful; drink, drugs, sex, sports, fraternities, and television are not. There are,
however, in each generation of students a few, a pitiful few perhaps, who stand
out in different ways from the mass of their contemporaries. And it is on the size
and style of that small group that one's hopes and optimism are pinned.*
—John Sullivan, "Some Thoughts on Freedom,"
Texas Observer, *November 7, 1969*

The antiwar protests of the late 1960s were a real pickle for Presidents Lyndon Baines Johnson (LBJ) and Richard Nixon. To be fair, opposition to war was nothing new in America. Many wealthy, conservative landowners and businessmen had opposed abandoning the British Crown to fight in a revolution in the late eighteenth century, and thousands of southerners refused to fight for the Confederacy. In Texas, thirty-four citizens of German descent were slaughtered at the Nueces River for attempting to flee to Mexico to avoid Confederate conscription. And in east Texas, hundreds fled to the confines of the Big Thicket to escape the Civil War, and they remained there for the duration of the conflict. They resented what they believed was "a rich man's war, but a poor man's fight." Many Americans also spoke out against the War to End All Wars (World War I), the Second World War and the Korean War.

However, the level of opposition engendered by the Vietnam War was something new. In the first six months of 1969, there were over 120 bombings, attempted bombings and acts of arson at American high schools and colleges. Young American men were fleeing to Canada and elsewhere to avoid the draft, active duty troops in Vietnam were ignoring direct orders and, in Texas, three soldiers at Fort Hood (later known as the Fort Hood Three) refused to deploy to Vietnam as early as June 1966. Young Americans—and Americans, in general—had grown increasingly tired of the Vietnam War and were beginning to question the United States' rationale for being there. And this, again, was before news of the My Lai Massacre thundered across the AP Newswire on November 12, 1969.

The Nixon administration asininely bristled at the criticism it received for ignoring its chief campaign promise, which was to end the war in Vietnam. In fact, instead of examining its approach to the issue and the frightful objectives it was pursuing, the Nixon administration incessantly complained

Dean of Students Floyd Martine giving the November 13, 1969 antiwar protesters three minutes to disperse. News Service Supervisor Pat Murdock stands at his side, recording. *Courtesy of the University Archives, Texas State University.*

about the naysayers and labeled them communist sympathizers or Hanoi apologists. Instead of taking a hard look at its own policies, the Nixon brain trust began psychoanalyzing its harshest critics: American youth. Henry Kissinger, Nixon's secretary of state, thought of the protesting students as "spoiled children" who had been ruined by affluence and lax parental methods. In his memoirs, he suggested that the protesters "had been brought up by skeptics, relativists and psychiatrists" and "were rudderless in a world from which they demanded certainty without sacrifice."

Nixon's speechwriter, Ray Price, concurred with Kissinger, later describing the demonstrations as "the fashion at the time" and "the latest hula hoop."[6] Nixon's chief of staff, H.R. Haldeman, expanded on the notion. "There are people who want to get excited about something," Haldeman observed. "And they don't really give much of a darn what it is they're excited about. And they move from one cause to the next. They get fired up on Civil Rights, then on antiwar, then on ecology, and it moves from one thing to another."[7] If they saw it, a late October editorial in the *San Antonio Light* (titled "An Erosion of Spirit") was music to Nixon insiders' ears:

> *Something far more fundamental than national division over the war manifest itself in the Vietnam moratorium demonstrations.*
>
> *What was really spotlighted on the world stage, at least for those who have eyes to see, was only indirectly connected to the war.*
>
> *That something was the current condition of American spirit—and the diagnosis is poor.*
>
> *On display was a spirit of mental and moral softness which makes even sincere, well-meaning people easy victims for carefully calculated propaganda.*
>
> *It was a spirit springing from overfed selfishness and self-indulgence, in which the sacrifice for ideals is regarded as either corny nonsense or not worth the effort.*
>
> *It was a spirit that has become accustomed to the best of everything, while giving nothing or as little as possible in return.*
>
> *It was a spirit which shirks responsibility....It was a spirit of permissiveness and preoccupation with the denial of traditional values.*
>
> *It was a spirit which tolerates and even encourages pornography, debasement of the good, and glorification of the corrupt, in its books, motion pictures and on its stage.*
>
> *It was a spirit in which political leaders are able to present disloyalty as patriotism and aid to the enemy as common sense.*

It was a spirit in which the spirit of godliness and responsibility for the welfare of neighbors are in danger of becoming obsolete.

Altogether it was a spirit which our forefathers could neither imagine, nor tolerate.

Its cancerous spread, if continued, would spell the doom of what was once the proudest, strongest, most idealistic and blessed nation on the face of the earth.

In November 1969, Kissinger told Nixon that the protesting students suffered from metaphysical despair, and he dismissed their opposition to the war as a passing fancy. He said, "They have the leisure for self-pity and the education enabling them to focus it in a fashionable critique of the 'system.'"[8]

Initially, the Nixon administration assumed the entire antiwar effort could be boiled down to cowardice. Nixon believed the movement was fueled by conscription and critics of it, especially those who were subject to the draft. He was convinced that antiwar protesters were doing everything they could "to keep from getting their asses shot off." The White House also suggested that overseas communists may have been behind campus unrest, and Nixon staffers leaned on the CIA to prove links between overseas operatives and student activists. When no connections could be legitimately documented, the CIA tasked operatives to infiltrate antiwar organizations and wreak havoc.

In the end, Nixon and the majority of his administration sought explanations for the burgeoning antiwar sentiment in every place aside from their own duplicity and malfeasance. The only staffers who had a sense of what was happening were largely ignored. National Security senior staff member Roger Morris (who resigned in April 1970 after Nixon ordered the Cambodian Campaign) lamented the White House's approach:

It's one thing to say that this presents a political problem and it may translate into votes down the line. It's another thing to say that, "Look, these people in the streets are thoughtful, they may have a point about the war, it may behoove us to rethink some of our assumptions." [The Nixon administration] never did that. They thought [the protesters] were insubstantial and capricious, they thought it was basically a draft protest, they thought they were cowardly, they thought they were there for frivolous reasons.... They just never took the protest serious in an intellectual sense.[9]

Texas State antiwar protesters at the November 13, 1969 Vietnam Moratorium. Paul Cates is seated upper left, holding a sign. Student Senator Kent Garrett is next to him, on the right with his arms crossed. Terry McCabe is sitting front left with his head turned and hands clasped on his shin. *Courtesy of the University Archives, Texas State University.*

White House aide Tom Whitehead was also ahead of the curve: "We simply have to face the fact that we have large numbers of extremely well-informed young people who are well educated and who think for themselves; that they tend to [be] overly idealistic and unrealistic does not alter the fact."[10]

The Nixon administration's inability to transcend its own tunnel vision was unfortunate but not surprising. Recent revelations indicate that Lyndon B. Johnson attempted to establish a peace agreement with North Vietnam in late 1968—just before the approaching presidential election—but Nixon torpedoed his efforts with an early October Surprise.[11] Nixon ordered Republican operatives to contact the South Vietnamese government through back channels and instruct them to reject the peace agreement. Then, though he was campaigning on a promise to end the conflict, Nixon doubled down on extending it, displaying no interest in ceasing hostilities. He was obsessed with power, and a withdrawal would have signaled weakness. He felt the same way about the protests—he couldn't afford to look weak.

The San Marcos 10 are cordoned off and surrounded by cowboys and jocks. *Courtesy of the University Archives, Texas State University.*

Shows of cavalier resolve and brash fortitude worked when the protesters were wild outliers, perpetrating violence, vandalizing property and scandalizing the antiwar message. Nixon was keenly aware of how much his administration benefitted from the rambunctiousness and lawlessness of the radical elements of the antiwar movement. In fact, in one of Nixon's innumerous monologues to aides and staff members, Nixon suggested that if radicals attempted to engage the vice president, Spiro Agnew, he should "go stand in front of the sign with the worst obscenity" scrawled on it. "If the Vice President were slightly roughed up by those thugs," Nixon confided, "nothing better could happen for our cause. If anyone so much as brushes against Mrs. Agnew, tell her to fall down."

The October 15, 1969 Moratorium would turn out to be something entirely different, though. The protesters wound up looking more like the adults in the room than the children. Nancy Zaroulis and Gerald Sullivan put it best in their book, *Who Spoke Up? American Protest Against the War in Vietnam 1963–1975*:

Vietnam Moratorium Day was peaceably observed by millions of Americans in thousands of cities, towns and villages across the nation. Historians at the Library of Congress told reporters what the young organizers of the event knew well, that it was unique in American history, the largest public protest ever on a national scale. But the special quality of the day went deeper. A Whitmanesque[12] alchemy was at work; a gentle spirit of comradely acceptance pervaded gatherings large and small where every shade of dissent was represented. For some, long kept in silent restraint by radical usurpation of the ground they might have taken, it was, at last, a chance to be safely heard. Only a few minor incidents of violence were reported, and these, as often as not, involved the presence of anti-demonstration hecklers. There were no ugly mob scenes; instead, in town after town, there were silent, reproachful vigils, endless reading of the names of the Americans killed in the war, candlelight processions, church services, and, in some cities, larger meetings where politicians spoke in muted terms. The extremes of citizen opposition to the war were come together, and whatever radical impulse strayed about the fringes of these gatherings was submerged in a spirit of civic solidarity and common enterprise.

Over two million Americans protested across the country on October 15, 1969, and it cast the entire antiwar movement in a different light. The second Moratorium to End the War in Vietnam in mid-November promised more of the same.

3

FIRST TEXAS STATE UNIVERSITY "MOBE"

In '68 many people assumed that since Nixon got elected the war would wind down or end. He had all this rhetoric about a plan in his pocket and what not, but just the reverse happened. Nixon just seemed to heat it up. By '69 it became apparent that the new administration wasn't going to end the war and if there was going to be a stop, it was going to have to come from the people. The campuses were a natural place for activism and consciousness to come into fruition. Southwest Texas was just not willing to deal with it. Southwest Texas was just a sleepy old campus—these kinds of things happened somewhere else.
—*Joe Saranello, quoted in the May 1989 issue of the* Hillside Scene

The first antiwar mobilization at Texas State University was part of the October 15 Vietnam Moratorium Day. Texas State senior Juan R. Palomo[13] had read about the planned moratorium events in a news magazine and thought "it might be a good idea to have something similar in San Marcos to coincide with the nationwide observances." He discussed it with his roommate, Terry McCabe, and McCabe agreed.

A Texas State Who's Who honoree in math that year, McCabe mentioned the idea to Joe Saranello, a new student from New York, and Al Johannes, a local religious leader. They both expressed interest. Members of the small group subsequently met at the Coffee House[14] and talked the idea over. They decided to hold a local moratorium on Wednesday, October 15, and McCabe and Saranello began making plans for it.

They sought and received the university's permission to have the gathering at the *Fighting Stallions* statue. Initially, the moratorium was only going to involve a demonstration at the statue, but the event grew. "A two or three-hour rally and demonstration against the war was originally planned," Saranello told the *College Star* at the time. "But due to the importance of this event, it is hoped that it will develop into an all-day affair, with a silent protest vigil on the grass after the speakers finish." The informal schedule also came to include a forum with several speakers inside the Fine Arts Auditorium and a teach-in at the Campus Christian Community (CCC) facility. McCabe rounded up several speakers, including Dr. William C. Pool (history professor), Dr. Daniel E. Farlow (assistant professor of government), Walter A. Winsett (English instructor), Jose Hinojosa (government instructor) and Reverend William Thomas Jr. of the CCC.

At an Associated Student Government meeting held on Monday, October 13, 1969, student senator and *Star* editorial cartoonist Kent Garrett introduced a resolution to support students' right to miss class and attend the

Texas State students participating in the October 15, 1969 Vietnam Moratorium. Frances Vykoukal is strumming a guitar center left, and Sallie Ann Satagaj is holding a sign that reads, "How Many Dead Will It Take?" *From the 1970* Pedagog *yearbook.*

October 15 moratorium event without penalty from their professors. The resolution failed, but the Student Senate did issue a statement:

> *We, the members of the Associated Students, feel that anyone wanting to participate in local actions concerning U.S. involvement* [in Vietnam] *on October 15, 1969, should be able to do so without penalty or prejudice.*

The demonstration planners circulated handbills announcing the sit-in, noting that it was part of a national effort and indicating that its purpose was "to show the government that the American people want an end to this tragic war—NOW!" The handbills also addressed the "penalty or prejudice" participants might suffer: "If you cannot get permission to leave class on October 15, then consider that an American soldier is somewhere lying in the mud in Vietnam, and he is our soldier—Is one unexcused cut too big a price to pay?"

The chairman of the executive council of the Texas State Young Republicans Club, Lee Wimberley Jr., penned a response in the *Dove's Right Wing*, the club's official newsletter. In it, he referred to the sit-in as a "strike" and claimed that supporting it would be equivalent to "signing a blank check against anything" the antiwar protesters opposed. Wimberley also urged Texas State students to "ATTEND CLASSES ON OCTOBER 15 AND SUPPORT NATIONAL GOVERNMENT."

The October 15, 1969 Moratorium began at the base of the *Fighting Stallions* statue between the Evans Academic Center and the Fine Arts Buildings at 10:00 a.m. Approximately three hundred students gathered for the protest; many of them carried peace symbol placards and others, including Frances Vykoukal, arrived with guitars strapped over their shoulders. Hundreds of students looked on, some supportive, others antagonistic. The demonstrators draped an American flag over one of the mustangs and carried handmade signs featuring antiwar slogans. Sallie Ann Satagaj's sign read, "How Many Dead Will It Take?" Other placards said things like, "Anti-Vietnam Is Not Anti-American," "Save Lives, Not Face," "War Kills, Peace Builds" and "Bring the Troops Home Now!" Several hecklers (whom the *College Star* referred to as "campus cowboys") brandished competing placards. One offered the standard pro-war retort "America: Love It or Leave It." Another sign advised antiwar protesters to "Support the G.I. not the V.C." Perennial Texas State activist John Pfeffer, a navy veteran of the Korean War, told Bill Cunningham, the *Star* reporter covering the event, "We're supporting the G.I.s, too. We just have different ideas on how to support them."

As the demonstrators performed guitar-accompanied sing-alongs of Bob Dylan's classic "Blowin' in the Wind"[15] and Dick Holler's popular ode to assassinated American icons, "Abraham, Martin and John,"[16] hecklers shouted obscenities and told them to "Get the hell out of San Marcos!" Then, one pro-war cowboy tried to pull rank, and it backfired. Shouting at one of the clean-cut antiwar demonstrators, the heckler said, "You been in the army yet, buddy?" The target of the taunt addressed his antagonist directly: "Yeah, I've been in for six years. What's it to you, son?" The surprised cowboy responded by charging to the fore of the pro-war onlookers, throwing his hat down in frustration and attempting to rebuke his perceived adversary in a "violent" fashion. At this point, Dean of Students Floyd Martine emerged from the pro-war assembly and "hastened" the overzealous cowboy back to the rear of the throng, warning the antiwar demonstrators that similar outbursts would lead to a cancellation of the event.

As the pro-war assembly continued to jeer the demonstrators, Vietnam veteran and transfer student Sidney Lupu stepped out of the crowd of onlookers and defended the moratorium participants. "Why didn't you come prepared?" he asked the hecklers, eliciting cheers from the antiwar demonstrators. At 11:00 a.m., the demonstration moved into the Fine Arts Auditorium, and an "overflow" crowd listened to the lineup of speakers intently. Dr. Pool suggested that President Nixon had no idea what he was doing and called the Vietnam War "immoral and unjust." Hinojosa discussed the disproportional deleterious effects the war was having on minority groups and posed a frequently unaddressed query: "How can we even pretend to help the people of South Vietnam when we can't even help our own?" Reverend Charles Gielow, the new director of the Catholic Student Organization (formerly known as the Newman Club), was an unscheduled speaker and called the moratorium a "wonderful day in American history" that eloquently emphasized its singular purpose. "We are here to express our deep weariness," he said, "with the never, never ending bloodshed."

After the short indoor rally, the moratorium participants returned to the base of the *Fighting Stallions* statue and resumed the sit-in. Martine promptly instructed them to remove the American flag they had draped over the statues and to "go have lunch." Then, he withdrew campus security. The demonstrators ignored Martine, but some expressed concerns that, since they were no longer protected by campus security, the pro-war hecklers might resort to a physical confrontation to disrupt the moratorium. Bob

Several Texas State students holding peace signs and taking part in the October 15, 1969 Vietnam Moratorium at the base of the *Fighting Stallions* statue. *From the 1970* Pedagog *yearbook.*

Barton, a local businessman and publisher of the *Hays County Free Press*, directly engaged the most vocal critics of the demonstration and politely calmed anxious elements on both sides of the issue.

At 1:00 p.m., the demonstrators began to make their exit, cleaning the area at the foot of the *Fighting Stallions* statue as they departed. Only one piece of evidence indicating that there had been a protest at the spot remained: the "America: Love It or Leave It" sign. A member of the pro-war congregation had left it behind, but an antiwar good Samaritan had taken it upon themselves to correct the glaring false dilemma[17] by inscribing a third option at the bottom of the placard: "Or Improve It."

Later in the day, some of the demonstrators attended the teach-in at the CCC, and others caravanned to Austin to take part in a larger antiwar rally being held at the state capital.

The day after the October 15 Moratorium, the Texas State Agriculture Shop caught on fire, and several of the "hippies" that campus cowboys had hurled profanities at the day before helped them extinguish the conflagration. In fact, when the fire threatened to spread to the maintenance building next door, one of the organizers of the moratorium event climbed up to the structure's roof to help a fireman stabilize the firehose.

Wimberley student and cowboy Alvin Corb's remarks regarding his antiwar classmates' response to the fire were recorded by the *College Star*. "I want you to say something about these hippies," Corb said. "They were down there fighting an Agricultural Department fire. Everyone was working together. That's the way it ought to be. That's the way we really should feel, anyway."

Alvin Corb's praiseworthy sentiment was not widely shared.

4

FIRST TEXAS STATE UNIVERSITY MOBE'S FOES

War is the health of the State.
It automatically sets in motion throughout society those irresistible forces for
uniformity, for passionate co-operation with the Government in coercing into
obedience the minority groups and individuals which lack the larger herd sense.
The machinery of government sets and enforces drastic penalties, the minorities
are either intimidated into silence or brought slowly around by a subtle process of
persuasion which may seem to them to really be converting them....But in general,
the nation in war-time attains a uniformity of feeling, a hierarchy of values,
culminated at the undisputed apex of the State ideal, which could not possibly be
produced through any other agency than war.
—Randolph Bourne, *"War Is the Health of the State," 1918*

The pro-war congregation that was present at the first Texas State Moratorium had not acquitted itself well; the moratorium faction had flatly ignored Dean Martine's instructions to vacate their spot at the base of the *Fighting Stallions* statue (shy of their 1:00 p.m. deadline), and the antiwar forces at the university, in general, had carried the day. They had easily garnered more support than they had had going into the event. To the powers that be—LBJ loyalists, Nixon supporters and the pro-war contingent at large—this was unacceptable, and they made little effort to conceal their dismay.

Over the next few weeks, numerous students aired their complaints in the "Reader's Pulse" section of the *College Star*. Peter F. Ellis suggested that the

American flag draped over the *Fighting Stallions* statue at the October 15, 1969 Vietnam Moratorium at Texas State. *Courtesy of the University Archives, Texas State University.*

moratorium aided North Vietnam, because it gave Hanoi a "good reason to hope that the American people may force the U.S. to withdraw." This was an increasingly effective talking point for the Nixon administration. When the president wasn't claiming the American antiwar movement was actually funded and coordinated by overseas communists (a supposition he, again, had tasked the CIA with justifying), he claimed that it was derailing U.S. foreign policy.

Texas State student James R. Bryson complained that the American flag that had been draped across the *Fighting Stallions* statue had been mistreated through an improper display and removal (he claimed the flag was bundled up instead of folded when the demonstrators took it down). Texas State student Kyle C. Brookshier called the moratorium a "flop" and condemned the *Star*'s "obvious misguided support" of the event. Several students denounced the *Star* for its lack of objectivity and intelligence.

Other letters, which were written in support of the sit-in, commented on some of the alarming machinations the administration was up to in response to the protest. In "'Dove' Proclaims Rally Misjudged," Sallie Ann Satagaj took Brookshier's characterization of the demonstration as a "flop" to task:

> *An action's success is based on the achievement of its objectives. The demonstration on this campus was a localized participation in the nationwide moratorium whose objectives were to display vividly before our President the vast numbers in the country who oppose the War and to influence President Nixon to take more decisive actions towards bringing the war to an end.... The main objective on this campus could be judged as being successfully fulfilled, because students were given a chance to express themselves* [on these issues].

Texas State student Mary Alice Kiker[18] raised concerns about university retaliations in "Leaders Warned":

> *Though the moratorium in protest of the Vietnam War ended only a few short hours ago, I have already heard of a number of students in positions of leadership across campus that are running the risk of losing their jobs for participating in this demonstration. Though I, as an unbiased (in either direction) student did not participate in the sit-in, I am appalled that the positions and respect of members of either group could be threatened.... The point to me is not whether we get out of Vietnam. The point is, having an opinion is a guaranteed right and to think that it could hurt a person's position or job status is terrifying.*

A third letter was sent in by a "Concerned Counselor":

Concerning the Moratorium, an issue has been raised, which, as concerned students, we feel should not be allowed to go unquestioned. The administration yesterday instructed the head resident of at least one dorm to have the dormitory proctors obtain the names of professors who allowed students to attend the Moratorium during scheduled class hours. As a counselor in a freshman dorm, I received this information from the proctor on my floor, and I feel that this action on the part of the administration constitutes an infringement of academic freedom of concerned professors. The essence of a representative democracy lies in the ability of citizens to responsibly question and debate issues concerning our government's foreign and domestic policies. The purpose of a university is to train its students to become active participants in this democratic system. Therefore, we feel that a professor who believed that his students should experience this aspect of our society should not be subject to administrative condemnation. The Moratorium yesterday was attended by students and professors who supported both sides of the issue and was, as it was intended to be, a recognition of the fact that our government is a government of concerned people. Therefore, we feel that the administration is unjustified in attempting to single out those professors who have an active concern for the future of these students and for our society.

Kent Garrett received an unsigned note that said, "No more anti-Vietnam cartoons—or else." The editor of the *Star*, Steve Blackmon, was also threatened by a pro-war Vietnam veteran and repeatedly accosted by other pro-war elements on the Quad. One critic of the publication suggested that a student newspaper should refrain from publishing commentary on any events that do not take place on campus. Another animated antagonist cornered Blackmon for several minutes, resorting to profanity-laced shouts (after his contentions were dismantled), before telling the editor he should be sent to Vietnam himself for even questioning the morality of the conflict.

There is no evidence that students who supported the war faced threats, harassment or serious repercussions from Texas State administrators, but just a few days after Sidney Lupu stepped forward to defend the October 15 Moratorium participants' right to protest, he was pulled out of one of his classes and informed that Dean Martine wanted to see him. After dropping out of junior college on the East Coast, Lupu was drafted and served in Vietnam from 1965 to 1967. He was discharged at Fort Hood, which gave him Texas residency.

History professor William C. Pool addresses an October 15, 1969 moratorium audience. Behind him, *from left to right*, are Jose Hinojosa, Terry McCabe, Joe Saranello, Walter A. Winsett, Daniel E. Farlow and William Thomas. *From the 1970* Pedagog *yearbook.*

He got married and worked for a while before becoming enrolled at Texas State in the fall semester of 1969 (on academic probation due to his aborted junior college attempt a few years earlier). Lupu[19] recalled:

> *Mr. Martine said he'd heard I was involved in a protest. He told me that that was not the way they did things around there. And he made sure to remind me that I was on academic probation, and that meant I could be dismissed at any time. I was working on a 3.8 or 3.9 GPA at that point, but it was my first semester back. So, I cooled my jets and that was the end of it.*

5
ANTI-PROTEST PROTEST

It's silly talking about how many years we will have to spend in the jungles of Vietnam when we could pave the whole country and put parking stripes on it and still be home for Christmas.
—*Ronald Reagan, interview with the* Fresno Bee *on October 10, 1965*

Most chroniclers of campus life at Texas State suggest that the student body was consistently tame in terms of activism until 1969. They mention a demonstration against university president James H. McCrocklin during the spring semester of that year as a general starting point for student protests in San Marcos, but this contention is shaky, especially if you spend a few hours perusing the pages of the weekly *College Star* (now the daily *University Star*) from the 1960s. As early as 1965, San Marcos 10 protester David Bayless—who first enrolled at the school during the fall semester of 1964 but was apolitical at the time—recalls some activist grumblings. Certainly, by late 1965, dissident voices were beginning to be heard or at least noticed, and one of them belonged to an assistant professor in the History Department: Bill C. Malone.

In the summer of 1965, Huntsville, Texas, was a hotbed of civil rights activity. Reportedly coordinated by activists from Beaumont and Houston, a group called Huntsville Action for Youth (also known as HA-YOU) began demonstrating around the town, specifically advocating for speedier integration (opening all Huntsville businesses to African Americans) and more equitable pay for black workers in the community and at the local

Sam Houston State College (now Sam Houston State University). In mid-July, they demonstrated every night for a week, picketing around the Walker County Courthouse and staging sit-ins at cafés and eateries to force local "whites-only" restaurateurs to serve them.

On Sunday, July 25, 1969, Martin Luther King Jr.'s former aide, Reverend Alfred A. Sampson (the assistant director of affiliates for King's Southern Christian Leadership Conference), spoke at a two-hundred-person rally at Huntsville's Emancipation Park. "We are serving notice on Huntsville and the state of Texas," Sampson said. "We are not going to let anyone turn us around." Afterward, two dozen civil rights demonstrators, all Caucasians, were arrested for disturbing the peace at Café Raven, an unintegrated local restaurant. As they spent that evening in the Walker County jail, black demonstrators marched outside, singing freedom songs and protesting their white cohorts' arrests. The following morning, most of the arrested demonstrators posted the $200 bond requirement and were released. A number were identified as students, professors and faculty members, including several from the University of Texas and Texas State. The jailed demonstrators from Texas State were Malone, Agriculture Instructor Frank Pinkerton and a student named Wayne Oakes.[20]

The sit-ins and demonstrations continued, and on August 13, 1965, Houston Reverend Bill Lawson spoke to civil rights activists on the Walker County courthouse lawn. "If you have to face violence," Lawson said, "just remember that the blood in the streets will finally clean up Huntsville, which has nothing more than a penitentiary and a second-class college." Members of the Houston KKK eventually descended on the community, and there were reports of violence against black demonstrators perpetrated by local police officers and Texas Rangers.

By early October, more restaurants and businesses in Huntsville were integrated, but not much had changed at the local schools. On October 2, three pupils from an all-black school were expelled for donning HA-YOU sweatshirts. On October 4, seventeen students from another all-black school were expelled for wearing HA-YOU sweatshirts. On the following day, five more were expelled. In mid-October, three dozen young black protesters were arrested for picketing outside all-black Sam Houston High School and holding a demonstration in the lobby of the Walker County courthouse—they were carrying signs that condemned the actions of school officials and the school board. Once incarcerated, several of the protesters chanted, sang and shouted in their cells for almost two days straight. They also trashed cell windows, window screens and cell bunk bedding in protest. On Wednesday, October 27, Walker County judge Amos A. Gates deemed nine of the Sam

Texas State students participating in the October 15, 1969 Vietnam Moratorium (Jackson Hall can be seen in the background). *From the 1970* Pedagog *yearbook.*

Houston High School demonstrators juvenile delinquents for habitually violating Huntsville city ordinances and sentenced them to indefinite terms in state schools. Six girls were sent to the Crockett State School for Girls and three boys were sent to the Gatesville School for Boys.[21] On Thursday, October 28, civil rights demonstrators appeared at two corners of the Walker County courthouse square to protest the sentences of the teenage demonstrators from the day before.

On December 1, 1965, the *Hays County Citizen* reported that, in a November 19 meeting, Malone was informed by Dr. Cecil Hahn, the head of the Texas State History Department, that he and President McCrocklin felt that Malone's off-campus activities could be detrimental to his upward mobility. Under the front-page headline, "Academic Freedom Questioned: Malone Is Warned," the December 3, 1965 edition of the *College Star* reported on the *Hays County Citizen* article, adding that McCrocklin and Hahn told Malone "that his participation in Civil Rights demonstrations in Huntsville last summer would seriously injure his chances for advancement." In recent interviews, Malone claimed Hahn went even further. "He said I better watch my step," Malone said, "that my pay raises might be jeopardized. And he hinted that I might be happier if I was someplace else."

The *Star* also noted that the fact that Malone had been recently involved in the planning and formation of a fledgling, statewide Liberal Party was "thought to bear considerable weight in the warning." The story also indicated that Malone himself had declined to comment on the coverage but stated that the article was factual. "The organizers of this new Liberal Party asked me if I would be the chairman and go to the upcoming Democratic Convention [in Houston]," Malone recalled. "I foolishly agreed. I was strictly a figurehead, but it put me in the limelight, again, and not in a good way where the college was concerned."

The same edition of the *Star* that reported on Malone's warning was, generally speaking, dominated by pro-war coverage. In fact, directly under the "Malone Is Warned" piece, a story titled "Students Back LBJ" announced that two student organizations were taking steps to demonstrate student and faculty support for Lyndon B. Johnson's leadership in regards to the conflict in Southeast Asia. Then, a page-two main editorial titled "The Torch a Fad?" took a jab at antiwar activists:

> *As was probably inevitable, the forms of protest against something or other that started out with the burning of draft cards is now being adopted by all kinds of nuts for all kinds of reasons.*

Somebody in St. Louis burned his library card in protest of an increase in the overdue book fine from three cents to five cents. He saved the ashes and mailed them to the mayor.

The other day, a student from the University of New Mexico burned his Social Security card to protest policies "which require one to work for a living."

This isn't the ultimate. We're waiting for somebody to burn his birth certificate to [protest] *having been brought into this vale of tears without his consent and being required to perform the involuntary act of breathing in and out all day long.*

It seems the torch has become a fad. We do not under any circumstances agree with the draft card burners, the marching protesters or the bearded beatniks who disagree with the Johnson Administration's policy in Viet Nam [sic]. *However, we would be the last one* [sic] *to say that these protesters do not have the right to do what they are doing.*

In the free and democratic society in which Americans exist, the protesters and card burners are the best example of what freedom really is. Just try protesting the government's policy in a communist nation.

Considering a similar page-two main editorial the month before ("Supporting the War Effort," which was published on November 5), a pattern was obviously emerging:

Within the last few weeks, American college students have seen a paradox in the actions of their fellow students. One group of students has demonstrated in support of the war in Viet Nam [sic] *while on the other hand another group has gone so far as to offer to send blood and supplies to the Viet Cong…*

One does not doubt the war protesters are American college students; they admit the fact as do we. However, we wonder if they are really American, American in the sense of love for country. Can these college students in all truthfulness call themselves Americans while at the same time supporting enemies of the United States? We think not.

We would be the last to call these Viet Cong supporters traitors, but no other word seems fitting to the situation. Like it or not, the United States is involved in a war and our government should command a unified war effort if we expect to win. We again would be the last to say that Americans don't have the right, yes even the duty, to protest the policies of the present administration if they disagree with them. This is their right. It is not their right, however, to support the enemies of the United States, not while American soldiers die in the jungles of Viet Nam [sic] *every day.*

The "Reader's Pulse" section of the December 3 edition of the *Star* echoed "Supporting the War" and "The Torch a Fad?" with a single long letter from Texas State student Pamela Reed. It, too, bemoaned antiwar voices at other universities before Reed concluded, "As a student of Southwest Texas State College, I am proud to know we have not had any such demonstrations."

Lest one get the idea that the *Star* was overdoing it in terms of its support for the war, it is worth mentioning a related incident that occurred in El Paso the day after the "Supporting the War Effort" editorial appeared. On November 6, 1965, Army Lieutenant Henry H. Howe Jr. joined thirteen civilians in El Paso in a picket line demonstration against the war, carrying a sign that read, "Let's Have More Than a 'Choice' Between Petty, Ignorant, Facists [*sic*] in 1968," on one side and "End Johnson's Facist

A Vietnam Peace Parade Committee poster requesting contributions for the victims of U.S. bombing in Southeast Asia. *Courtesy of the Library of Congress.*

[*sic*] Aggression in Vietnam" on the other. When the El Paso Police Department braced the protesters, Howe, who was dressed in plainclothes, told the officers he didn't have any identification. Howe was arrested on vagrancy charges, but during questioning, his military identification was discovered in one of his shoes. He was subsequently handed over to Fort Bliss authorities. It was the first publicized instance of military resistance during the Vietnam War.

The next edition of the *Star*, published on December 10, 1965, featured a front-page display of conservative orthodoxy, an attempt to downplay the Malone issue and news of a student activist group being formed. Though there is no accompanying story or location for the conservative activity indicated, the upper left-hand corner of the *Star* is devoted to a prominent photo of a clean-cut male student distributing "anti-protest protest" leaflets on campus. The story next to the image announced that the "Malone Problem Appears Solved." In it, readers learned that President McCrocklin was reported to have said a professor's outside political activities would have no effect upon his chances for promotion at this school. Speaking with the *Star* and the *Daily Texan* (the newspaper for the University of Texas), McCrocklin said, "As far as I'm concerned, it would not affect a man's chances for advancement." In the article, Dr. Hahn took full responsibility for the "warning" gaffe, stating that his previous cautionary remarks to Malone were only intended as "friendly advice." Though Malone had met with McCrocklin on November 22 and his request for a written statement detailing the school's promotion policy was refused, he expressed satisfaction with McCrocklin and Hahn's comments on the subject.

Malone recently clarified the matter. "He wouldn't promise me anything on the issues of promotion and tenure," Malone said. "And he also mentioned that he thought I'd been dressing rather slovenly—or words to that effect. I dressed casual. I almost never wore a suit and tie."

Below the "Malone Problem Appears Solved" report in the December 10, 1965 edition of the *Star*, a companion story titled "First on Campus: Student Group Forms" discussed what may have been one of the earliest acts of student activism at Texas State.[22] Co-chaired by Eddy Etheridge and Rob Robertson, the effort, called the Students' Committee for Professors' Rights, indicated that its purpose was to serve as a vehicle for disseminating "information concerning academic freedom" to the student body. Etheredge stated that the group's goal was to determine "who the originator of the warning to Dr. Malone was" and to procure a statement of repudiation from the party or parties responsible. The December 10, 1966 *Star* page-two main editorial on the subject ("On Academic Freedom") tried to have it both ways:

> In our opinion, the incident involving Dr. Malone and his troubles with the administration this week was not, in reality, a violation of academic freedom. We feel that because of misinformed sources, the story was allowed to get out of hand.
>
> It was for this reason that the Star declined to comment on the situation last week.
>
> However, the Star also feels that, although academic freedom was not violated in this manner, it was bruised sufficiently to warrant a statement from Dr. McCrocklin about his stand concerning a professor's outside political activities without fear of losing their jobs.
>
> It is also our belief that a professor's contribution to the school and to the students should be the only criteria for promotion.

We will agree with Dr. McCrocklin that professors should enter into outside activities of the political, religious or civic nature. Some of these may be controversial, but if the individual involved gives of himself and does what he thinks is right, it is right.

In one of the first publicized instances of military resistance to the Vietnam War, Fort Bliss Army Lieutenant Henry H. Howe Jr. protested in El Paso on November 6, 1967. *Courtesy of the* El Paso Times.

"My department was split over the whole thing," Malone recalled. "Some said I was making a mountain out of a molehill, that I had just taken the words wrong and exaggerated the import of them, that nobody was really in jeopardy of anything." But the situation troubled Malone. "Things just sort of accelerated from there," he said. "I wanted to get away from the strife and struggle. I just decided maybe I ought to get out."

Seven months earlier, in the last regular *College Star* edition of the 1964–65 academic school year, published on May 14, 1965, President McCrocklin had been named the "Top Newsmaker" at Texas State by the *Star* staff, and the runner-up was the principal speaker at McCrocklin's November 20, 1964 inauguration, President Lyndon B. Johnson himself. In the coming years, other professors and instructors would test the parameters of academic freedom and integrity on campus and find them arbitrary. In the meantime, however, President McCrocklin—especially in relation to LBJ—could not afford to be seen as overtly oppressive or retaliatory, so the Malone issue was tamped down for the time being.

On December 19, 1965, Lieutenant Howe was court-martialed. Though his participation in the November 6 protest did not violate army regulations, he was convicted of "conduct unbecoming an officer" and "using contemptuous words against the President." On December 22, he was sentenced to two years' hard labor; his sentence was later reduced to one year.

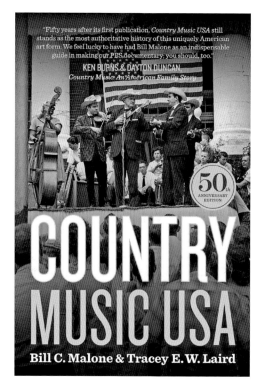

Embattled Texas State instructor Bill C. Malone went on to teach at Tulane University and write the most popular book on American country music ever published. *Courtesy of Mr. Malone.*

Malone would eventually leave Texas State and go to Murray State University in Kentucky, the University of Wisconsin at Whitewater and Tulane University, where he retired Professor Emeritus. He remains a noted musician, author and historian, and his 1968 book, *Country Music, USA,* became the first definitive academic history of country music in America.

If student activism threatened to stir at Texas State in 1965, it seemed to doze through 1966. In the May 6, 1966 edition of the *College Star,* a page-two main editorial titled "It Is Our War" says it all:

> *It was less than a month ago when President Lyndon B. Johnson was told by campus administrative and student leaders that Southwest Texas had, as of then, experienced no protests over the Viet Nam* [sic] *War. This week, the President would have been sorely disappointed as members of the Students*

for a Democratic Society from the University of Texas distributed anti-war literature and asked for American withdrawal from Viet Nam [sic].

These protesters believe that the Viet Nam War is wrong because it is "politically disastrous, economically suicidal and morally outrageous." And their literature is slanted to prove this position.

Anti-war demonstrations and protests bring to mind a question that we hear more frequently these days. "Is it our war?"…Deep down we know the answer is yes, it is our war. It is our war as surely as the bullets fired by both sides are real and deadly.

War is always a personal thing. And the current conflict in Southeast Asia is no exception as both belligerence and hysteria grip the American public. The President has spoken often of "winning the war." We fear that wars of the present type can no longer be won clearly and simply on the battlefield or in the rice paddies.

To win, America must be firm with its Asian allies and bomb when necessary to facilitate the war's progress, but we must never fear the negotiations table. And most of all, the United States must never reject its avowed policy of maintaining peace throughout the world, through military might if necessary.

If anyone has the duty to protest, it is the American patriot who never makes the headlines but who dies so that protesters like SDS members are free to do whatever they wish. We don't object to their right to protest, but we certainly do object to their cause.

Less than two months later, three American soldiers at Fort Hood (just one hundred miles up the road in Killeen) refused their orders to deploy to Vietnam. Dubbed the "Fort Hood Three," twenty-year-old Private Dennis Mora and twenty-five-year-old Private First Class James Johnson Jr., both of New York, along with twenty-year-old Private David A. Samas of Modesto, California, issued a statement regarding their decision on June 30, 1966:

We represent, in our backgrounds, a cross section of the army and of America. James Johnson is a Negro, David Samas is of Lithuanian and Italian parents, and Dennis Mora is a Puerto Rican. We speak as American soldiers.

We have been in the army long enough to know that we are not the only G.I.s who feel as we do. Large numbers of men in the service either do not understand this war or are against it. When we entered the army, Vietnam was, for us, only a newspaper box score of G.I.s and Viet Cong killed or wounded. We were all against it in one way or another, but we were willing to "go along with the program"…but, later on, Vietnam became a fact of life when someone you knew wondered how he could break the news to his girl, wife or family that he was being sent there. After he solved that problem, he had to find a reason [for going] that would satisfy him. The reasons were many. "Somebody's got to do it," "When your number's up, your number's up,"…"The pay is good," and, "You've got to stop them someplace," were phrases heard in the barracks and mess hall, and used by soldiers to encourage each other to accept the war as their own. Besides, what could be done about it anyway? Orders are orders…

No one used the word "winning" anymore because in Vietnam it has no meaning.…The three of us, while stationed together, talked a lot and found we thought alike on one overriding issue—the war in Vietnam must be stopped. It was all talk and we had no intentions of getting into trouble and making waves at that stage.

Once back in Texas, we were told that we were on levy to Vietnam. All we had discussed and thought about was now real. It was time for us to quit talking and decide. Go to Vietnam and ignore the truth or stand and fight for what we know is right.

We have made our decision. We will not be a part of this unjust, immoral, and illegal war. We want no part of a war of extermination. We oppose the criminal waste of American lives and resources. We refuse to go to Vietnam!

This was the first occasion of American GIs refusing to deploy during the Vietnam War, but—whether because it happened over the summer when the main student body was gone or because the *Star* wasn't printed over the summers—there doesn't seem to have been much discussion about it at Texas State around the time of the incident or after students returned to school.

Later that year, in a two-day Professor Discussion Series (held November 7–8), which was sponsored by the Student Union and headlined by the *Star* afterward as "Profs Disagree Over Viet Nam," Texas State assistant professor of government Dr. Weldon V. Barton and Dr. Bernard Fall, a Howard University professor of international affairs, largely agreed on almost everything. The event was made out to be a serious, substantial debate, but it was actually insubstantial and uncontroversial.

Dr. Barton observed that we couldn't win in Vietnam in any military sense but neither could the Viet Cong or the North Vietnamese. Dr. Fall countered that the United States could win militarily in Vietnam, but that it wasn't really worth it because our "militaristic aspects" were "totally useless" in this type of guerrilla warfare. Barton and Fall both detailed quagmires and stalemates where no one came out on top, and each conceded that negotiations were probably the best answer; but they both also suggested that a victory in Vietnam would not halt "Communist aggression and expansion in Southeast Asia." The only notable statement that was made was a strange throw-away, tack-on quip that Dr. Fall probably should have led with: "War doesn't stop anything," he said. "There are more guerillas fighting in the Philippines, Thailand and Venezuela than in Viet Nam [*sic*]."

In the April 13, 1967 edition of *The Record*, a "Marine's Vietnam Diary" entry from Private First Class George Kreiner (who was stationed in Dong Ha, Vietnam) commented on the Fort Hood Three:[23]

> *I returned Saturday morning, prepared for a long wait. I had two novels and a two-weeks-old paper from New York. After reading a news story about the war, I opened the paper to a half-page ad for the Fort Hood Three—three draftees who refused to go to Vietnam because they believe this is an immoral war. After reading their reasons, I felt sure they were wrong in their convictions, yet I felt it was wrong to send them to jail (two of them are serving five years and the other one is serving three years of hard labor).*
>
> *I know that discipline is an essential factor in the make-up of a good fighting force. But it is un-American to send a man to jail because he refused to commit what he believes is a crime against humanity.*
>
> *The fact that they did not abandon their principles when confronted by a five-year prison term proves they are not the cowards that many people call them.*

In 1967, student activism at Texas State was still sparse, especially during the spring semester, but the issue of academic freedom once again emerged, this time with the added controversy of a threat to free speech.

In 1965, Dr. William I. Gorden, a Texas State associate professor of speech and director of forensics (the debate team), had begun including a radio panel discussion program in some of his classes. Participating students initiated and taped open conversations about a number of contemporary issues, and the recordings would later be aired on radio stations around San

Henry Kissinger, President Richard Nixon and Major General Alexander Haig discuss the Vietnam War during a meeting at Camp David. *National Archives and Records Administration.*

Marcos and New Braunfels. One program even dealt with hallucinogenic drug experimentation.

On March 20, 1967, four of Dr. Gorden's pupils taped a conversation devoted to the "sexual revolution." Though the informal commentary involved three girls and one boy and excluded obscene language, a representative from KCNY in San Marcos, one of the local radio stations that usually aired the conversations, contacted the chairman of the Journalism Department, Dr. Bruce Roche, and told him the program was risqué. Roche explained to Dr. Gorden that the students needed to re-tape the discussion with less "marginal" remarks. Dr. Gorden spoke with the original participants and arranged for three of them to revisit the subject. On March 22, however, Roche contacted Gorden again and told him that the re-taping was scrapped. President McCrocklin was in possession of the original recording, and the program had been cancelled. In an April 28, 1967 front-page exposé titled "Sex and the College President," the *Texas Observer* shared a description of the taped conversation provided by *College Star* editor Porter Sparkman, who had heard the recording himself:

In [the] *opening statements, a girl on the program said today's younger generation knows that sex is not just once a week in the marriage bed but that it's good anytime, anywhere, and all you need is fifteen minutes. The boy said he had it and he likes it. One of the students referred to making love in the "missionary position." A girl said the college is known by its graduates and has a legitimate interest in some regulation of student sex. Availability and education in the use of contraceptives were discussed. Pro-sex developments at the University of Texas were discussed, evidently without an excess of accuracy. Statistics from the Kinsey report and information from* Playboy [magazine] *had a role on the program. "Contraceptives was about the worst thing they said," Sparkman said. "How many letters is that?" His point was that the worst thing they did was use a fourteen-letter word. He said he wouldn't have said some of the things that were said, but if they wanted to say them, "Ok." In general, two of the four students were very enthusiastic for the new morality and extra-marital sex, one of the girls indicated she wasn't for this sort of thing, and the third girl said she thought it's a matter of individual judgment.*

The conversation appears to have been relatively harmless but controversial for the times.

Prior to the incident, Dr. Gorden had been on a tenure track at Texas State, but this changed very quickly. College officials informed Dr. Gorden that his promotion to full professorship had been suspended by President McCrocklin pending an investigation by administrators. He was also informed that future panel discussions were to be confined to the classroom. Dr. Gorden said they were overreacting and that he was uncomfortable with explaining the situation to his students, because, in effect, he was being forced to take sides. Gorden also defended the taped conversation, essentially noting that, even if the panelists weren't experts, the language was colloquial and the subject matter, though vulgar to some, still included authentic dialogue with intellectual value and should not be suppressed.

Dr. Gorden wrote a letter regarding the issue to the central Texas chapter of the ACLU, and, on March 30, 1967, George Schatzki, the president of the chapter and a University of Texas law professor, along with Reverend John A. Hurd Jr., the chairman of the chapter's academic freedom committee, responded. They informed Gorden that, according to their interpretation of the events, infringements of academic freedom and free speech were involved and they were interested in the case.

By then, however, Gorden had been increasingly disturbed by the proceedings and felt his somewhat unconventional approach to academics and his own students was going to be used against him to argue that he lacked maturity, which may have created further complications. "My department chair sided with President McCrocklin," Gorden said in a recent interview. "He was no longer going to back me and my professorship wasn't going to go through."

Ignoring Reverend Hurd's urging to stay the course and consider legal action, Dr. Gorden tendered his resignation at Texas State on April 11, 1967. He subsequently told the *Observer* that "the restriction of his students' discussion to the classroom deprived them of valuable learning experiences, alienated them, retreated from faith in dialogue, and put the college in a position of defending controlled speech." He told the *Star* that he simply "couldn't work under a climate of censure." By the fall semester of 1968, Dr. Gorden was teaching at Kent State University in Ohio, but the immediate effects of the controversy at Texas State brought attention to something even more nefarious.

Mike Holman participating at the November 13, 1969 Vietnam Moratorium at Texas State. Al Henson can be seen in the background, just over Holman's left shoulder. *Courtesy of the University Archives, Texas State University.*

When the *Texas Observer* interviewed Sparkman about the incident, he said that when he had first heard about the cancellation of the radio broadcast, Lillian Dees, the Journalism Department secretary, telephoned him. During that phone call, Dees informed Sparkman that, according to Dr. Billy J. Hinton, dean of the School of the Applied Arts, if Sparkman reported on the incident at all, he'd be fired. While Sparkman was putting the final touches on the next edition of the *Star*, journalism instructor Kenneth Casstevens checked in, reminding him that Dr. Hinton didn't want anything printed on the subject.

The following week, Sparkman contacted President McCrocklin directly and told him that members of the *Star* staff were "really upset" about the way the incident was being handled and particularly with the restrictions on coverage. McCrocklin quickly assured Sparkman that the whole thing had been a mistake. Sparkman told the *Observer* that McCrocklin said he "was free to publicize the case, and that what had happened had been due to a misunderstanding—that he, McCrocklin, had told Hinton to go and freeze the tape, but not to stop publication of the news in the student paper." However, Sparkman[24] also mentioned a "Johnson restriction" in his interview with the *Observer*. He indicated that upon his election to the editorship of the *Star*, the journalism chairman informed him that the newspaper was "prohibited from editorializing on any of President Johnson's policies." When the *Observer* brought this issue up with McCrocklin, he "appeared surprised, and a vice president of the college, who was sitting in on the interview, appeared absolutely astonished."

———

By the time the fall semester of 1967 rolled around, the Gorden affair was mostly quashed on campus, and when the thing that most pro-war sorts dreaded most threatened to occur at Texas State, Dean Martine quashed that as well.

Almost two years to the day before the first Vietnam Moratorium, another incident took place at the Student Center. On October 17, 1967, David Massey, a graduate student from Bryan, Texas, and Thomas Wilson, a senior from Studio City, California, approached Martine and procured a permit to distribute antiwar materials on campus the following day. Martine issued the requested permit.

According to the October 20, 1967 edition of the *College Star*, Massey and Wilson set up "headquarters" in front of the Student Center at approximately 8:00 a.m. on Wednesday, October 18. The antiwar materials, which were provided by the University of Texas Committee to End the War in Vietnam, comprised a small selection of pamphlets that criticized the war and the U.S. presence in Southeast Asia. Massey and Wilson were soon joined by Barron Holloway, a senior from Waycross, Georgia, and the three chatted with passing students while handing out pamphlets. The antiwar pamphlet distributors attracted a small audience of the sympathetic and curious until around noon. By then, pro-war passersby were beginning to congregate, grow angry and protest. Some of the antiwar-protest protesters had relatives fighting in Vietnam. The husband of one blonde coed, who openly challenged Massey, Wilson and Holloway, was currently deployed. Frustrated pro-war onlooker Cliff Berkman, a junior from Victoria, Texas, came up with a plan to stop Massey, Wilson and Holloway. Soon, he and other supporters of the war approached the antiwar trio to peaceably ask them for some of their pamphlets. But instead of taking the antiwar literature and perusing it or going on their way, Berkman and his friends began dropping the pamphlets into a pile on the steps of the Student Center. In a matter of moments, the discarded antiwar literature was ignited and engulfed in flames. The *Star* story on the incident referred to the conflagration as a "small bonfire."

Word of the confrontation and the pamphlet-burning was communicated to the students of the University of Texas who had provided Massey and Wilson with some of their literature later that evening, and on the following afternoon, ten to twelve of them caravanned to Texas State on motorcycles. According to the October 20, 1967 edition of the *Austin American-Statesman*, under the headline "SWT Rejects UT Peaceniks," the University of Texas contingent apparently met with Martine at the "Lair" in the Student Center to inquire as to why Texas State students couldn't protest the Vietnam War. While sipping coffee and surrounded by a small mob of two hundred pro-war Texas State students, Martine was curt and dismissive. "The college issued a one-day permit for distribution of the literature," Martine informed the UT visitors. "The great majority of our students were not sympathetic with it and burned it."

"Another permit has not been issued," Martine continued. "I am sure you would not want to break college rules by attempting any sort of demonstration. I am sure you will follow the rules of our school as we would respect the rules at UT." One leather-jacketed University of Texas student

Satagaj, Bayless and Murray Rosenwasser participating in an antiwar sit-in on November 13, 1969. *Courtesy of the University Archives, Texas State University.*

responded. "I guess if any San Marcos students want to protest the killing in Vietnam, they'd better come up to Austin," he said.

"Do you have any more questions?" Martine quipped. Another University of Texas student answered: "Yes. How do we get out of here?" As the group from the University of Texas turned to leave, Martine's two-hundred-student entourage cheered. The *Statesman* later noted that Martine's "smooth handling" had prevented a confrontation.

In the October 20, 1967 edition of the *College Star*, two pro-war letters featured in the "Reader's Pulse" section condemned the original, permitted antiwar trio. The first was from Daryl W. Tumbleson:

> *I've often heard of anti-war demonstrations happening at large universities but have never* [seen it] *on this campus. Since I just returned from a year in Viet Nam* [sic] *I'd like to express my viewpoint and that of my friends who died fighting.*
>
> *My entire outfit—the 101st Airborne—was firmly convinced that America is obligated to help any free peoples' government resist Communism when they cannot help themselves. If we let the Communists have South Viet Nam* [sic]*, we might as well let them have the rest of Southeast Asia.*

The people who stage peace demonstrations are freeloading on freedom. They want to enjoy the freedom of living in the United States, but they don't want to defend it. These Peaceniks protest freely and openly, yet if we permitted the Communists to overtake any country that they choose, then someday these kooks wouldn't have the right to protest anything.

One eighteen-year-old paratrooper actually cried when he learned of a peace movement at his high school. He died in combat sick at heart to think that his ex-classmates protested the cause he believed in so deeply.

The demonstrators are saying that our young men are being forced to fight. I lived and fought with dozens who gave their lives fighting....I can say that in every way they believed in the cause for which they died.

At a service in memoriam to these men, our chaplain quoted Abraham Lincoln in saying: "What they have given is far beyond our power to add or detract." I ask you, Barron Holloway, David Massie [sic] and Tom Wilson, what have you done to earn the freedom you enjoy in America today?[25]

The second letter was from the engineer of the antiwar literature bonfire himself, Cliff Berkman:

TO ALL THE PEOPLE OF SLEEPY HOLLOW AND ALL POINTS SOUTH:

Well, babies, it's finally happened. Southwest Texas State College, that "Friendly College on the Hill," has finally been invaded by the Anti-Vietnam Movement. Some of us were privileged to witness this "Happening." Too bad that Lyndon wasn't here to see his Alma Mater shine so brightly! (In a way I'm glad he wasn't, for there were enough of us sick at our stomachs as it was, and I for one would really have hated to see our Commander in Chief wretch and heave in a puddle).

Literature (if you can call such dribble literature) was displayed for a short time. Some of it was even passed out. It grew quite chilly all of a sudden, and I decided to build a fire. This dribble burned much better than it read. There was talk of adding fuel in the form of bodies to the flames, but no immediate action was taken. They just don't make SWT cowboys like they used to.

The entire "demonstration" was a joke to some, and as usual the "protesters" were the biggest joke of all, merely stooges for some bigger "pinko." Like some philosopher once said, "Fools name and fools faces."[26]

To some of us, however, this was no more of a joke than the war itself. To any one of us who have ever lost a buddie [sic], a brother or a father in the jungles of Viet Nam [sic], *it was a slap in the face, an open insult. It irks me to know that my friends and yours are dying and fighting so these "protestors" can pass out this dribble and deface their memories.*

If these protestors are so eager to gain an audience, why not set them up a booth in front of Fort Polk[27] or Camp Pendlton [sic]*.[28] I'll be glad to personally provide transportation for all of them who wish to go.*

Berkman concluded the letter by identifying himself as "An American, and Damned proud of it."

In the editorial section of the October 27, 1967 edition of the *College Star*, it initially appeared that the pro-war elements at the university might carry the day again. Political editor Chuck Hanson condemned the recent antiwar demonstrations around the country and criticized them for devolving into acts of oafish defiance. In an editorial titled "Open Resistance Predicted," Hanson likened antiwar protesters to cornered animals resorting to more and more desperate measures because they sense the "growing tide against them." In the accompanying "Reader's Pulse" section, however, several concerned parties addressed the instances of antiwar activism that occurred at Texas State the week previous, and surprisingly—or alarmingly, depending on your perspective of the issue—most of the responses defended the protesters. There were, of course, some exceptions. The Young Republicans on campus were quick to address the "peaceniks," but even they were critical of how the war was being handled:

We, as members of the SWT Young Republicans Club, would like to state our opinion about the recent occurrences on our campus concerning the South East Asia policy of the United States. In answer to the "peaceniks" on our campus, who feel we must pull out of Viet Nam [sic] *at any cost, we say American troops are presently meeting the threat of International Communism in Viet Nam* [sic]*. While we support the basic military action now being taken, we believe the present policy to be lacking in determination to achieve victory. We urge that the United States use every reasonable means for the successful completion of this war.*

The letter was signed by several Young Republicans Club officers, including Lee Wimberley Jr.,[29] who would later criticize the Vietnam Moratoriums.

Pro-war sign after a clause had been added at the bottom by a good Samaritan at the October 15, 1969 Vietnam Moratorium at Texas State. *From the 1970 Pedagog yearbook.*

A small, local alumni group also chimed in, lauding the pro-war protesters:

> *The Exes of SWT who are teaching at Canyon High School wish to commend the students of SWT for the action they took against the students from Texas University[30] when they appeared in protest against the war in Viet Nam* [sic]*.*
>
> *We feel that so long as we have men and women who are as brave and loyal as those students, we have no fear for the safety of our country.*
>
> *Thanks to them for handling this situation with so much acumen and success.*

The letter was signed by eighteen Canyon High educators.

While there was a lot of support for the pro-war protesters, a letter from another off-campus party, Glenn Schulze, dispelled the notion of pro-war bravery and loyalty in the recent engagements:

> *To all the cowboys, frat-rats, et al, so eager to stand up for America, SWT, Dean Martin,[31] LBJ, Mom and apple pie:*
>
> *You sure were a brave bunch against three students voicing their own, hard-thought opinions on the war and nine non-students who wouldn't have fought with you for any reason and had no desire to cause trouble.*
>
> *I wonder if you would have been so brave last Saturday when 1,500 Americans marched to show their disfavor of the war. We received no hassle from the spectators and only two people bothered to show up at the rally to voice their support of the war.*
>
> *A recent national poll has estimated that about 46 percent of the American people are against the war. This is almost one-half! The movement extends far beyond the Haight-Ashbury.[32]*
>
> *I propose that you "git on yore hoss and ride west"—and east and north and south. Look around you. There are people doing a lot of thinking and they are not going to stand in the shadows. There is also something called freedom of speech, which allows a person to voice his opinion. Granted, this is a dangerous thing—but freedom of speech limited is freedom of speech denied.*
>
> *You may not agree with us, but listen—you might find out something. "And you know that something's happening and you don't know what it is, do you—Mr. Jones."[33]*

Mr. Schulze's sentiment presaged the San Marcos 10.

Texas State students staging a Vietnam moratorium sit-in at the base of the *Fighting Stallions* statue on November 13, 1969. Huddled front right are Joe Saranello and Frances Vykoukal. *Courtesy of the University Archives, Texas State University.*

One letter from an anonymous writer celebrated a break in the general obliviousness their fellow students displayed in terms of the larger issues facing them and the nation as a whole:

> *FLASH! IT FINALLY HAPPENED! SOMEONE AT SOUTHWEST TEXAS SCHOOL OF MEDIOCRITY AND APATHY FINALLY EXPRESSED AN OPINION ON A CONTROVERSIAL ISSUE!*
>
> *Far be it from the administration to get involved directly, but, through their sanctions, two students actually acquired permission and set up a booth to distribute material disagreeing with current U.S. policy concerned with this war.*
>
> *Though this writer must DISAGREE with their methods and what they advocate, I extend my support to them for being able to break out of the Establishment Doldrums and at least actively show how they feel.*
>
> *And how bravely and democratically our super patriots here responded. It is a rare day when you can see such a moving sight as a mob of Rexall*

Cowpersons and general flunkies surround three drama students and shout "pinko" and a few other words they have heard somewhere.

It must have made them feel real brave to condemn people for exercising a right that our friends in Viet Nam [sic] are fighting to keep, namely the basis of democracy, freedom of speech and the right to your own opinion.

Freshman Trey South echoed the anonymous writer's views:

Part of the trouble comes from the habit of majorities. These people seem to think that if more people believe in what they do then all others must be wrong. They refuse to see or even listen to the other side's opinion.

In the letter from Daryl Tumbleson, he asked the demonstrators what they had ever done to earn the freedom they enjoy in the U.S. . . . They have a right to disagree, whether it deviates from what you believe or not. You give the impression that just because you've been to Viet Nam [sic] and think everyone should be eager to go, and they're not, then they don't deserve to live in the United States. How narrow-minded can a person be?

Richard B. Henderson Jr., son of the chair of the Government Department, Dr. Richard B. Henderson, perhaps put it best when he said:

Does being an American mean that we should follow every law, policy and cause of our government like sheep following the herd? Doesn't being an American also consist of exercising the right to dissent if we do not agree with the majority?

I personally am not strongly for or strongly against the war in Viet Nam [sic]. I don't think I know enough about the situation to defend either position, and I don't believe that enough people do. Too many of us have based our views on emotion without any objective study of the situation.

The treatment of the antiwar protesters on our campus was deplorable. As I understand it, they had gained permission to pass out their literature in advance and were orderly. The fact that they were in a very small minority and their opinions were not very popular on this campus does not mean that their rights should not have been respected. How can a strong argument be built concerning any issue without listening to both sides of it? Why are you so afraid to allow the other side to present their opinions?

America would not be the great country it is today if none had ever questioned the ruling majority. All or part of a minority opinion may be found to be valid or, in most cases, useful in strengthening the majority opinion. We would not have our free society if we had nothing but apathy and blind loyalty.

I am not a peacenik (I tried to enlist in the armed forces two years ago and was rejected due to a physical defect), nor do I identify with them, but I feel that someone should defend their right to protest just as strongly as others have defended the war in Viet Nam [sic].

The irony of both Tumbleson's and Berkman's pro-war letters to the *College Star* on October 20 is that both seemed to be condemning Massey, Wilson and Holloway for actually attempting to "earn the freedom" they enjoy in their country. Tumbleson alludes to the soldiers in Vietnam fighting and dying for the freedoms Americans enjoy. Among those, of course, is the right to free speech, ergo, the right to protest. What both Tumbleson and Berkman failed to grasp is that one of the fundamental ways a citizenry can demonstrate an appreciation for their rights, and therefore earn them, is by exercising

Texas State students protesting the Vietnam War at the base of the *Fighting Stallions* statue on October 15, 1969. *Courtesy of the University Archives, Texas State University.*

them—perhaps especially when their stance is unpopular. Berkman was only irked by his classmates' application of their First Amendment rights because he did not agree with them. Neither Berkman nor Tumbleson recognized that their interest in stopping, curbing or shouting down Massey, Wilson or Holloway much more resembled the tactics of a communist regime than those of the United States.

Most at issue, however, was Dean Martine's handling of the treatment of October 18, 1967 antiwar literature distributors. Two Texas State students went through the proper channels and secured a permit to distribute antiwar pamphlets. In retrospect, the actual protest that occurred was staged impromptu by the pro-war faction, and they didn't just confront the administration-sanctioned pamphlet sharers, they were involved in a physical confrontation and created a fire hazard, using the distributors' own documents, on the steps of the Student Center. Then, of course, the admitted arsonist suggested in the university newspaper that perhaps the permitted pamphlet sharers should have been tossed into the flames as well.

Dean Martine's response to this was only mildly shocking. He sided with the pro-war protesters who hadn't had a permit or permission to protest and then suggested the permitted pamphlet distributors had basically gotten what they deserved. "The students themselves just started burning the darn stuff," Martine told the *Star*. "Which I thought was very interesting." Martine didn't criticize the pro-war protesters or condemn the burning of antiwar literature, and there is no evidence that he ever cautioned or punished Berkman for torching the pamphlets, creating a fire hazard in broad daylight or teasing the immolation of the members of the antiwar trio. Then, the following day, two hundred pro-war students coincidentally showed up to help Dean Martine welcome the University of Texas students who traveled to San Marcos to inquire about the issue with Texas State students protesting the war. *Who informed the pro-war entourage that UT students were on their way?* Martine's behavior was obviously questionable, and it should be noted here that he hardly treated all protests—permitted or scheduled—the same. At the very least, the demonstrations and demonstrators who shared Martine's mindset clearly enjoyed more latitude.

In the spring semester of 1968—a few months after the pamphlet burning—Jerry Spencer, from Randolph Air Force Base, sent a letter to the editor of the *Star*, which was featured in its March 15, 1968 edition:

> *SWT in general, and* Star *in particular, are very distressing for a person trying to take an open-minded and intelligent stand on the Viet Nam* [sic] *crises.*

The campus is overly apathetic and what is not apathetic is ultra-right wing. The Star *could easily be mistaken for the "Voice of LBJ."*

I have done a fairly extensive amount of research into the South East Asian area and its problems since the Geneva Accords of 1964. I don't believe that anyone doing any similar examining could find it in himself to support LBJ's fruitless, wasteful and endless escalation as a solution to the crisis.

Why can't the Star *be more like other campus newspapers and present both sides on an intelligent basis instead of being used by the conservative faction that controls this campus? Cheap little attacks on...minority groups...don't serve any purpose but to show the true narrowmindedness and gross ignorance of the vast majority of students at SWT without examing* [sic] *the issues thoroughly enough to form an intelligent opinion.*

I think my point was backed up by the reception given those students last semester who tried to pass out "peace literature."

In the editorial section of the April 5, 1968 edition of the *Star*, editor Jan Albrecht announced the student newspaper's stand on Vietnam:

Let's get out of Vietnam. BUT LET'S GET OUT BY WINNING. *When we leave Vietnam, let's walk away with a signed peace treaty, not crawl away from a continuing war.*

6
SICK SOCIETY

A true war story is never moral. It does not instruct, nor encourage virtue, nor suggest models of proper human behavior, nor restrain men from doing the things men have always done. If a [war] story seems moral, do not believe it. If at the end of a war story you feel uplifted, or if you feel that some small bit of rectitude has been salvaged from the larger waste, then you have been made the victim of a very old and terrible lie. There is no rectitude whatsoever. There is no virtue. As a first rule of thumb, therefore, you can tell a true war story by its absolute and uncompromising allegiance to obscenity and evil.
—*Tim O'Brien,* The Things They Carried[34]

At the Riverside Church in New York City on April 4, 1967, Martin Luther King Jr. gave a speech titled "Beyond Vietnam: A Time to Break Silence." It is probably the thing that got him killed.

In the United States, Martin Luther King is widely celebrated as a civil rights champion, which he undeniably was, but he was also a profound antiwar voice—and this scared the powers and forces behind the American military-industrial complex. Three paragraphs of his broken silence on Vietnam follow:

> *Since I am a preacher by calling, I suppose it is not surprising that I have seven major reasons for bringing Vietnam into the field of my moral vision. There is, at the outset, a very obvious and almost facile connection between the war in Vietnam and the struggle I, and others, have been waging in*

America. A few years ago, there was a shining moment in that struggle.[35] *It seemed as if there was a real promise of hope for the poor—both black and white—through the poverty program. There were experiments, hopes, new beginnings. Then came the buildup in Vietnam, and I watched this program broken and eviscerated, as if it were some idle political plaything of a society gone mad on war, and I knew that America would never invest the necessary funds or energies in rehabilitation of its poor so long as adventures like Vietnam continued to draw men and skills and money like some demonic destructive suction tube. So, I was increasingly compelled to see the war as an enemy of the poor and to attack it as such.*

Perhaps a more tragic recognition of reality took place when it became clear to me that the war was doing far more than devastating the hopes of the poor at home. It was sending their sons and their brothers and their husbands to fight and to die in extraordinarily high proportions relative to the rest of the population. We were taking the black young men who had been crippled by our society and sending them eight thousand miles away to guarantee liberties in Southeast Asia which they had not found in southwest Georgia and east Harlem. And so we have been repeatedly faced with the cruel irony of watching Negro and white boys on TV screens as they kill and die together for a nation that has been unable to seat them together in the same schools. And so we watch them in brutal solidarity burning the huts of a poor village, but we realize that they would hardly live on the same block in Detroit. I could not be silent in the face of such cruel manipulation of the poor.

My third reason moves to an even deeper level of awareness, for it grows out of my experience in the ghettoes of the North over the last three years—especially the last three summers. As I have walked among the desperate, rejected, and angry young men, I have told them that Molotov cocktails and rifles would not solve their problems. I have tried to offer them my deepest compassion while maintaining my conviction that social change comes most meaningfully through nonviolent action. But they ask—and rightly so—what about Vietnam? They ask if our own nation wasn't using massive doses of violence to solve its problems, to bring about the changes it wanted. Their questions hit home, and I knew that I could never again raise my voice against the violence of the oppressed in the ghettos without having first spoken clearly to the greatest purveyor of violence in the world today—my own government. For the sake of those boys, for the sake of this government, for the sake of the hundreds of thousands trembling under our violence, I cannot be silent.

Civil rights champion and Vietnam War activist Dr. Martin Luther King Jr. was assassinated in Memphis, Tennessee, one year to the day after he gave a powerful antiwar speech at the Riverside Church in New York City. *Wikimedia Commons.*

In an April 6, 1967 editorial titled "A Tragedy," the *Washington Post* claimed the speech "diminished" Martin Luther King's "usefulness to his cause, to his country and to his people." In an April 7 editorial titled "Dr. King's Error," the *New York Times* condemned the speech, calling it slanderous and suggesting that in the "fusing of two public problems that are distinct and separate" Martin Luther King had "done a disservice to both." A year to the day after his "Beyond Vietnam" speech, Martin Luther King was assassinated in Memphis, Tennessee. There aren't many people familiar with the chronology of these events and the history of King's turn against the Vietnam War who believe this is a coincidence.

On Friday, April 5, 1968, the day after King was murdered, a small group of Texas State students, upset by the fact that the university's flags weren't flying at half-mast, mourned his death and commemorated his memory by protesting campus prejudice. First, they scrawled,[36] "When are you going to kill God?" (presumably in chalk) all over the Quad. Then, the informal spokesman, Austin junior Vernon Edwards, and nine other students—black and white—sat, sprawled and laid across the front steps of the Old Main administration building, creating a human barricade. The *Star* coverage of it captured some predictable responses:

The first noticeable reaction was expressed predominantly by non-students (secretaries and faculty members) as well as some students. They tried to ignore the show and, at times, discourage others from venting their reactions to the demonstration. Many hurried by [or up the steps of Old Main], *apparently oblivious to what was going on, stepping over and around Edwards and the other demonstrators.*

Then there were those who wanted to "put that nigger in his place." One pipe-smoking faculty member paused as he entered Old Main to give his opinion of the situation. "Get up and go work, and make something of yourself," he said. Other students threatened under whispers to handle the matter by force.[37]

The strange spectacle attracted a large crowd, and eventually, Dean Martine appeared, accompanied by Dean of Men Bobby Jarrett and James B. Hobbs, assistant to the president. But instead of giving the demonstrators three minutes to disperse, having the campus police cordon them off or threatening them with expulsion, Dean Martine asked the group to join him for a discussion of their issues and grievances in the shade of the adjacent Art Building porch area. The conversation lasted for an hour, and some faculty members joined in.

Edwards said the group was trying to bring attention to Dr. King's assassination and the racism displayed on campus, particularly the amount of bigotry that flew under the radar. "I'm saying that the majority of whites just won't do nothing about those whites who are bad," Edwards contended.

Martine was repeatedly put on the defensive in terms of explaining the treatment of blacks and black athletes and the university's habit of turning a blind eye to some of the well-known racist institutions on campus, but he parried skillfully. When chided over the lack of African American scholars in the school's faculty, Hobbs replied that the university had tried to hire more African American personnel but that they were hard to obtain due to their popularity around the state. Martine added that Texas Southern University[38] graduates were in high demand at colleges, universities and private businesses. When the administrators were questioned about the delay in lowering the flag to honor King's passing, Hobbs said that the university "had been waiting on official word from the federal government" and that the flag had been lowered around noon.

Edwards held his own. He railed against the condescending "integration" smiles that so many black students received from their white counterparts. He also criticized the de-emphasis of the accomplishments of exemplary

Texas State students created a human blockade in front of the entrance to Old Main on April 5, 1968, to protest the assassination of Martin Luther King Jr. and racism around the campus. *From the 1968* Pedagog *yearbook.*

African Americans like Nat Turner and Attorney General Thurgood Marshall,[39] and he dismissed a recent Texas State student exchange program with Prairie View A&M[40] as a "token" event. Then, according to the *Star* coverage of the exchange, Edwards concluded with a challenge: "I'd like to see the president of this college get up before the student body and say with no uncertain terms that he would not abide any act of racism on this campus whatsoever."

English instructor Stephanie Chernikowski said that people should no longer be viewing each other in terms of color. Dr. Alfred E. Borm,[41] an assistant professor of mathematics, went even further when he said, "I once felt I wasn't going to do penance for the sins of my grandfather. But now something...has made me see that I do owe something. [Martin Luther King] was fighting for all of us."

When Martine was later asked about his kid-glove handling of the demonstration and the protesters, he replied that "a little bit of sugar goes a lot farther than a barrel of vinegar." Though there is no evidence President McCrocklin ever spoke in any certain or uncertain terms about racism at Texas State, several students did take up the issue in the April 12, 1968 edition of the *College Star*. The page-two main editorials were devoted to the subject. The first, "March On!" encouraged a continued commitment to Dr. King's causes:

> *"If I were to die, I want you to be able to say that I tried to love and serve humility…if you want to say that I was a drum major, say that I was a drum major for justice. Say that I was a drum major for peace."*
>
> *The words in the preceding paragraph were part of a recent sermon. The man who spoke the words, Dr. Martin Luther King Jr., was shot to death by an unknown sniper Thursday, April 4.*
>
> *Dr. King's body was entombed Tuesday in a marble crypt enscribed with the epitaph, "Free at last, free at last, thank God Almighty, I'm free at last."*
>
> *More than 150,000 Americans, great and unknown, black and white, attended the funeral of the murdered civil rights leader. Thousands more across the nation mourned him at local memorial services and in the privacy of their homes.*
>
> *Dr. King is dead, but we hope that his words will continue to live and to guide Americans as they seek solutions to racial injustice. Martin Luther King was an advocate of justice and of peace. Our nation has much need of both of these qualities.*
>
> *The drum major is dead. Will the American band, the band of justice and peace, keep marching on?*

The second editorial, "Riots for Peace?" was more dire:

> *A man of peace died last week. Since then, men of violence have killed at least thirty-five other Americans, burned whole blocks to the ground and looted hundreds of stores. This they did in memory of Martin Luther King and in vengeance for his death.*
>
> *The man who died in Memphis last week was a leader in America's struggle for racial justice and peaceful advancement. His death was violent, but his life was spent in preaching a creed of non-violence. Would he be pleased with the memorial of smoldering ashes and hate created in his name?*
>
> *We talk about the war in Vietnam. What do we say about the war in America?*

Saturday, troops stood guard duty over buildings demolished by fires set by arsonists during a night of burning and pillaging. The troops and the burning were both in Washington. That night, guardsmen exchanged fire with snipers. The shots were fired in the streets of Chicago.

The discontented, both black and white, rioted their way across the nation. Some had legitimate reasons to complain of their lot; others were just bored.

The innocent, both black and white, died across the nation. Some were taking part in the rioting when they died; others just happened to be in the wrong place at the wrong time.

Is America already involved in a second civil war? If so, who is fighting whom and for what reasons? The rioters and arsonists who proclaimed the rule of anarchy this weekend did not fight for civil rights or equality before the law. They were not reformers; they were criminals.

Is America at war with itself? Perhaps. Perhaps the symbol of America today is not the Statue of Liberty or the Star Spangled Banner but rather the soldier in battle dress who stands watch, with bayonet fixed to his rifle, at the entrance to the White House.

A man of peace died last week. Will men of violence destroy the nation and the people, both black and white, for whom he gave his life? The question is one we must answer.

The "Reader's Pulse" letters section was primarily devoted to a discussion of King's assassination and secondarily to the Vietnam War, but they almost seem to blend and merge. Vernon Edwards wrote in, expanding on the comments he made in his discussion with Martine.

There seems to be a fatal quietness by the students of SWT about the problems before us all and a tragic air of aloofness about the plight of black men in America…and the struggle affects us all.

Students on this campus today must align themselves with and actively participate in the black movement that is sweeping the nation. The fact is that we cannot afford to sit back and accuse, blame or even "pass the buck," but we must unhesitatingly join and offer direction and leadership in the movement….

Racism is running rampant and unchecked throughout America from California to the Carolinas. In our national capital, in our statehouse, in our schools, on our streets and in our churches, we feed racism a goodly diet. And racism will continue to plague us until we meet it head on with force.

Vernon Edwards, the Texas State organizer of the April 5, 1968 demonstration following the assassination of Martin Luther King Jr. *From the 1968* Pedagog *yearbook.*

Texas State student Nick Thiele submitted a letter urging his classmates and fellow Americans to start thinking for themselves and become more involved in the issues that affected them:

> *It becomes more and more apparent each day that the United States has truly entered into what may be called a year of decision. With talks between North Vietnam and our nation concerning the possibility of peace in Southeast Asia close at hand, and with the murder of Dr. Martin Luther King having precipitated riots in Chicago, New York City, Washington, D.C., Baltimore and Memphis, we should see that the time has come for every American to become involved. If we intend to save the United States,*

and that Salvation is indeed dependent upon us, then we must get interested, we must act. Much about the U.S. is good and much more good could be realized if we would only begin to work toward that goal....

The hope of the nation is in its youth, and, if we decide to idly sit by and watch our nation be destroyed by our apathy and our contentedness, then we must accept the fall. If you truly love your country, you can't complacently sit and watch. You must think and you must act and you must do it now.

Texas State student Kathy Quanstrom seconded Thiele's notion:

The explosion spreading across our nation is the direct result of the inadequacies of our sick society. We are a people so involved in annihilating dissent that we have become totally blind to the reasons behind that growing frustration. We kill our leaders. We fight riots with tanks. We combat poverty and ignorance with empty promises and non-existent funds.

The solution is not easy; the answers, not simple. Direct action must be taken....

Minds and ideas cannot be changed immediately by laws—but they can be changed. Let's not stop with suggestions and recommendations and finish with tanks and sub-machine guns.

The most interesting letters came from U.S. soldiers who were still in service. The first is from former *Star* editor (1964–65) Edmond S. Komondosky (then a second lieutenant in Vietnam):

I am enclosing a copy of a poem that is currently circulating on post. I thought it might be of interest to some of you. As you may well remember, I am an old "hawk" of the LBJ brand from way back. As far as I know, there is no copyright or ban on publishing the poem if you so choose.

Take a man, put him alone,
Put him 12,000 miles away from home.
Empty his heart of all but blood,
Make him live in sweat and mud.
This is the life I too live,
And why my soul to the devil I give.
You peace boys rot in your easy chairs
But you don't know what it's like over here,
You have a ball without even trying

While over here your boys are dying.
You burn your draft cards, you march at dawn,
And plant your signs on the White House lawn,
Use your drugs, have more fun,
And then refuse to use the gun.
There's nothing else for you to do,
And I'm supposed to die for you?
I'll hate you 'til the day I die,
You made me hear my buddies cry.
I saw his arm a bloody shred,
I heard them say, "This one is dead."
It's a large price he had to pay
Not to live another day.
He had the guts to fight and die,
He paid the price, but what did he buy?
He bought your life by losing his
But who gives a damn what a soldier gives?
His wife does, parents and even sons,
But they're about the only ones.
You all want to ban the bomb,
And you say there is no war in Vietnam.
You try to hide the truth from all,
But everyone can see right through this wall.
So, who am I to fight for you?[42]

The second letter, another correspondence from Jerry Spencer at Randolph Air Force Base, took an entirely different and extraordinarily perceptive view:

Your "Stand on Vietnam" sounds like a cross between Richard Nixon and a John Bircher.[43]

First of all, let's agree on this. They (North Vietnam and Red China) are not going to run out of people, and the Soviet Union is not going to run out of arms to supply them with. In other words, they are able to carry on the war indefinitely. We cannot! Our dollar is now in grave danger. No country can afford $6 billion[44] *a year on war and remain in good shape. That is what your stand advocates.*

You say "get out of Vietnam by winning." What is your idea of winning—escalation until the Red Chinese are forced into a

Martin Luther King, Jr.'s Ten Commandments on Vietnam

1. Thou shalt not believe in a military victory.
2. Thou shalt not believe in a political victory.
3. Thou shalt not believe that the Vietnamese love us.
4. Thou shalt not believe that the Saigon Government has the support of the people.
5. Thou shalt not believe that the majority of the South Vietnamese look upon the Viet Cong as terrorists.
6. Thou shalt not believe the figures of killed enemies or killed Americans.
7. Thou shalt not believe that the generals know best.
8. Thou shalt not believe that the enemy's victory means Communism.
9. Thou shalt not believe that the world supports the United States.
10. Thou shalt not kill.

From an address given by Mrs. King on April 27, 1968.
Copyright © 1968 by Coretta Scott King.

Promoting Enduring Peace
P. O. Box 103
Woodmont, Conn. 06460   Additional copies FREE except for postage.   C-18

Martin Luther King Jr. condemned the U.S. war in Vietnam and called the government of his own country "the greatest purveyor of violence in the world today." *Courtesy of the University Archives, Texas State University.*

confrontation with us, or worse yet, the use of nuclear weapons? What is your idea of "peace"—our system and ideas or total destruction for that land and its people?

You point out that Johnson said nothing about a coalition government including the VC [Viet Cong]. Do you think the Communists will settle for less when that is what they originally began fighting for?

One fact should stand out: The U.S. (not allies) are the only foreign troops in Vietnam. Of course, Russia and Red China have "advisors" as we did before '64. This is one thing; taking on the bulk of the fighting and sacrifices for an admittedly "corrupt" dictatorship is quite another thing. We jumped into Vietnam and escalated unilaterally. That is how we should get out—unilaterally. If our government wishes to do as the Soviet Union does, and we did before 1964; that is, supply "our side" with arms and aid, all right. But we can no longer sustain the bulk of the fighting and sacrifices.

Another point is that Ho Chi Minh is a Nationalist Communist; but by war on him we force him closer to Peking—thus defeating our purpose of "stopping the Reds."

Communism did not work in Indonesia, the Middle East, Africa or South America; but some of us are sure it will work if we just get scared enough of it. The fear of the Commies, I feel, is being used to dupe the American public into supporting the war.

After King's assassination, five thousand active duty U.S. troops stationed at Fort Hood were shipped to Chicago with orders to discourage and, if necessary, put down riots. Several black civilians perished. In mid-August 1968, it was decided that another large number of GIs stationed at Killeen would return to Chicago in late August for riot-control duty at the Democratic National Convention. Around midnight on Friday, August 23, five dozen African American troops staged an orderly, nonviolent sit-in at the intersection of Sixty-Fifth Street and Central Avenue at Fort Hood to protest their deployment to Chicago. The majority of these soldiers had sincere and serious reservations about being put in a situation where they might be asked to engage other black Americans as hostiles. Several demonstrators mentioned that they had grown up in ghettoes and said they knew why people were rioting. "The people we are supposed to control, the rioters, are probably our own race," one protester said. "We shouldn't have to go out there and do wrong to our own people." Another African American soldier explained their perspective by saying, "Most of them have seen action. They have done the job they have been trained to do. And we were sent back here to Ft. Hood to control the situation in the streets. We—the black soldiers at Ft. Hood, the ones who are aware—are not going."

Around five o'clock on Saturday morning, the first armored division commander and members of his staff met with the protesters and spoke with the group for approximately one hour. Seventeen of the demonstrators dispersed, but forty-three remained. Those men were immediately placed in the base stockade for failing to report for morning reveille. Some reports indicated they were beaten along the way.

These protesting soldiers became known as the "Fort Hood 43," and their refusal to board a plane to Chicago for riot-control duty was one of the largest acts of dissent in U.S. military history. Over the next few months, several of the Fort Hood 43 were court-martialed and punished, receiving sentences of three to six months of hard labor, a forfeiture of two-thirds of their wages and reductions of rank across the board.

In late September 1968, a U.S. House-Senate conference committee added a special rider[45] to one of Lyndon B. Johnson's higher education bills. It stipulated that college administrators could begin denying financial aid to students who participate in campus "disorders."

7

McCROCKLIN DEBACLE

In his letter of December 28, Harry Drucker asks:
Where is the patriotic spirit "my country right or wrong?"
In a speech in 1918, Theodore Roosevelt stated "…to stand by the President,
right or wrong, is not only unpatriotic and servile,
but it is morally treasonable to the American people."
It was this "blind patriotism" that led the Germans to start World War II,
and it is this same kind of patriotism that will lead us to World War III
if we are not careful.
—*Juan R. Palomo, "Letter to the Editor,"*
San Antonio Express, *January 1, 1968*

I f the first six months of 1968 at Texas State were challenging due to issues raised by events off campus or in other parts of the country, the final six months were rocky due to an on-campus narrative that would shake the university to its foundations.

Not long after James H. McCrocklin took over as the fourth president of the school on November 20, 1964, the *San Antonio Express* did a nice piece on him titled "McCrocklin Brings Dynamism to SWTSC." It even included a good-sized image of McCrocklin holding a copy of one of his seven books, *The Making of the Modern World*. The *Express* attributed the simultaneity of McCrocklin's prolific writing, his performance as a three-term mayor of Kingsville and his job as a teacher at Texas A&I College (now Texas A&M University) to his exceptional work ethic and energy. He had also served as president of both the Texas Municipal League and the Texas Association of College Teachers and, before all of that, had achieved the rank of captain in the Marine Corps and lieutenant colonel in the Marine Corps Reserve and received his bachelor's degree, master's degree and PhD at the University of Texas. The *Express* was clearly impressed:

> *McCrocklin is something of a surprise to those who harbor stereotyped images of college professors and presidents. He is six feet, two and weighs 230 pounds. He still sports a Marine crew-cut, and drives around the hilly campus in an El Camino pickup.....Neither an absent-minded or ivory-tower type, he works with the speed and dispatch of a corporation executive.*

McCrocklin was happy to expound on the secrets to his success. "I think you have to make decisions quickly," McCrocklin told the *Express*. "You complicate the situation by delaying."

When questioned about navigating city politics and dealing with the local commissioners as the mayor of Kingsville, McCrocklin said he tried to work toward a consensus. "If you are going to have dissension," he added, "you should not have it publicly." When asked how he found time to write with everything else he had going on, McCrocklin replied "The answer is 'you don't.' You make it. You set a time and go to work." President McCrocklin seemed a like a real down-to-earth go-getter—except this overachieving "everyman" had friends in high places.

In 1962, President McCrocklin was a campaign manager for Lieutenant Governor Preston Smith and a coordinator for John Connally's successful gubernatorial campaign. He also seemed to have a special connection with LBJ. Floyd Martine told the Texas State student magazine *Hillside Scene* in 1990, "McCrocklin was one of LBJ's favorites....Johnson thought McCrocklin was *the* man. And he was. He was very influential in getting a lot of recognition for the college." Johnson spoke at McCrocklin's inauguration, and he signed his first Higher Education Act (increasing the amount of federal money given to universities to create scholarships, establish low-interest loans for students and create a National Teachers Corps) at Texas State on November 8, 1965.[46] Johnson also chose McCrocklin to serve on the National Advisory Committee on Selective Service in 1966 and named him to an eighteen-person CIA committee tasked with reviewing the "recommendations of a government panel that investigated financing of schools and other groups" in 1967. Then, Johnson made McCrocklin the undersecretary of the U.S. Department of Health, Education and Welfare

University president James H. McCrocklin in his office at Texas State University. *From the 1966* Pedagog *yearbook.*

in late July 1968, and he was scheduled to remain the number-two person at that agency until Johnson left office on January 20, 1969. Meanwhile, in McCrocklin's four-year tenure, Texas State's enrollment doubled, the infrastructure of the university was expanded and upgraded and the institution acquired a federal fish hatchery. Johnson had a lot to do with these developments, but they still occurred on McCrocklin's watch.

Before McCrocklin left to assume the undersecretary position, his parting words probably filled many students and faculty members with pride. "So there will be no confusion in anyone's mind," McCrocklin said, "I intend to take the assignment in Washington as an honor bestowed upon our institution. On January 21 [1969], I intend to bring that honor back to this campus." However, as *Hillside Scene*'s student journalist Scott Ritter[47] noted in 1990, "Unfortunately, McCrocklin's return was distinguished by something altogether removed from honor."

The seeds for the institutional cataclysm that was to come at Texas State were planted in 1964. In the 1960s, the Republican Party wielded very little power in Texas, but a progressive contingent within the historically conservative Democratic Party was beginning to make strides. In 1964, two Texas State instructors, John Quincy Adams (also an attorney) and Charles Chandler, were part of that progressive effort. Earlier, Adams, a supporter of the local NAACP group, and Chandler had wrested the chairmanship of the Hays County election precinct from the sitting mayor by garnering support from a largely untapped constituency: the local Mexican American and African American populations. The growing progressive wing of the Democratic Party was narrowly defeated in the Hays County Democratic convention in 1964, and plenty of conservative, establishment Democrats were furious with Adams and Chandler. According to a 1986 interview with longtime, respected Texas State professor Daniel E. Farlow (who was at the 1964 convention), the only reason the establishment Democrats carried the day that year was because President McCrocklin had been present and "some of the faculty people [involved in the convention] felt intimidated and switched their votes so that his side won."[48]

In 1965—despite the fact that several instructors (and faculty members) with master's degrees were routinely teaching at Texas State well past the three-year allotted span they received to complete their doctorate—Adams was told his contract would not be renewed at the end of the academic year because he had not finished his doctoral requirements. Adams informed President McCrocklin that although his doctoral work was not complete, all he lacked was his dissertation, which he was in the middle of finishing. He asked President McCrocklin to be permitted to remain an additional year (with no chance of retention afterward) so that he could finish the final research for his dissertation and have time to search for another position. McCrocklin denied his request and suggested he resign. The contemporary newspaper reports implied Adams left of his own accord.

When the *Texas Observer* later questioned President McCrocklin about his refusal to give Adams a one-year extension, McCrocklin denied that Adams had been asked to resign, indicating that his contract was not renewed because he "had in the meantime resigned on his own." Adams corrected the record in a recent interview. "I didn't resign," he said. "I received a one-year terminal contract with only nine months notice, which is something they weren't allowed to do. But I didn't know any better at that time."

Chandler would later experience a similar fate, and there was no small number of Texas State faculty members who believed Chandler and Adams were targeted for serving up something of a headache for the conservative wing of the Democratic Party in Hays County. In fact, it was generally believed that McCrocklin was simply executing an errand for that faction. Adams took his lumps and accepted a post as a visiting professor at Millsaps College in Mississippi. "It wasn't long before Millsaps wanted me to stay permanently," he said. Popular and well-respected, Adams remained there for twenty-nine years.

Chandler wound up at Texas Tech University in Lubbock, but he had friends at McCrocklin's former university, Texas A&I College. There had always been whispers about McCrocklin's academic pedigree in south Texas. Textbook salesmen who plied the university circuit in that region occasionally mentioned rumors about Mr. and Mrs. (Harriet) McCrocklin's scholarly writings. The specifics of the gossip are unknown, but an examination of Dr. McCrocklin's published works is useful. Though McCrocklin was credited as the author of seven books in the November 20, 1964 *San Antonio Express* article, the only volume he appeared to have actually written (at the time) was the one that sprang from his dissertation: *A Study of the Garde d'Haiti, 1915–1934*. The others were all revisions of older works.

McCrocklin's *Building Citizenship* was originally written by Ray Osgood Hughes in 1933 and copyrighted by him in 1946. *The Making of Today's World*, which McCrocklin holds in the *Express* feature photo, was written by Hughes in 1935 and also copyrighted by the original author in 1946. Hughes saw several reprintings of *The Making of Today's World* and then it was revised by C.H.W. Pullen and reprinted in 1956. McCrocklin isn't involved in a revision until 1963. Hughes also saw several reprints of *Building Citizenship* before a new addition appeared in 1957, revised, again, by Pullen. McCrocklin's revision was published in 1961. Then, McCrocklin was credited for revisions of related teacher's manuals and test guides (i.e., *Tests for Hughes and Pullen's the Making of Today's World*, 1964, which was only forty-eight pages long) and answers to tests guides (i.e., *Answers and Tests Accompanying Hughes and Pullen's The Making of Today's World*, 1962, which was only thirty pages long). Beyond being revisions of revisions, however, McCrocklin's offerings were also, apparently, notably unimpressive. When reviewed in the Cambridge University Press's *History of Education Quarterly* in 1968, McCrocklin's *The Making of Today's World* was panned. The Fairleigh Dickinson University reviewer, Bernard Reiner, was rather blunt:

> *Alas, after 771 tedious pages narrative, maps, and pictures, what emerges is not the broad view of human civilization but an old-fashioned indelicate*

defense of the use of American political and military power....America is seen as the land of the free, and it took twenty disorganized units [chapters] to prove this point....Facts are used merely to support a prior conclusion.... The book is intended to make American students more comfortable with their past history and to help them understand the country's role in the modern political theatre....Maybe the sins of the father should not be revisited upon the son, but there was no other way of reviewing this senseless book.

In light of these insights, characterizing McCrocklin as the author of seven books arguably becomes a stretch. And at some point during the resulting conversations regarding the aforementioned aggrieved victims of the conservative wing of the Democratic Party at Texas State, talk of looking into the McCrocklins' dissertations emerges. In interviews conducted with Chandler by email with Texas State master's candidate Shae R. Luther in 2006 and 2007, Chandler revealed that he had received a copy of Mrs. McCrocklin's thesis from friends at Texas A&I in the summer or fall of 1965 while conducting interviews for his own dissertation in Kingsville. Chandler then checked out a copy of Mr. McCrocklin's dissertation from UT and began examining them side by side. He found "many long sections of supposedly original text that were identical." With proof that the rumors were true and that plagiarism was obvious, Chandler held an "open house" at his home in San Marcos, displaying the McCrocklin manuscripts for other faculty and staff members "to view and make up their own minds as to whether plagiarism had occurred." Chandler also told Luther that he was surprised by the number of friends, associates and "people from all parts of the college" (including some he suspected represented McCrocklin's interests) who came by to examine the papers.

When Chandler was informed that his contract at Texas State would not be renewed beyond the spring of 1966, he applied for a position as an instructor at Texas A&I College, but (perhaps unsurprisingly, because McCrocklin still had so many connections there) his application was rejected. According to his interviews with Luther, Chandler claimed "one of McCrocklin's minions" later tried to sabotage his eventual position at Texas Tech by identifying him as a "dangerous communist," but his new department head "laughed it off."

In late 1966, Chandler's wife, Carolyn, who happened to be a journalist employed by *The Cedar Chopper's Almanack* (which, at the time, proclaimed itself "Hays County's Only News Magazine"), published a story on McCrocklin's plagiarism, but the *Almanack* had limited readership and the

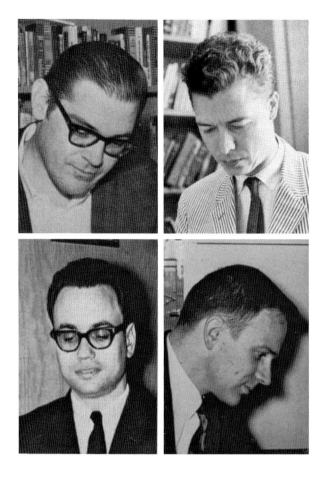

Young instructors (*clockwise, from top left*) Bill C. Malone, Charles Chandler, John Quincy Adams and Dr. William I. Gorden all encountered serious conservative opposition at Texas State. *From the* Pedagog *yearbook*.

original article has proven difficult to locate. Farlow mentions the article in his 1986 interview, indicating that "it caused all kinds of excitement and division on campus," but nary a word of it appears in the *College Star* or the more established area newspapers of the time. It was not until Friday, August 9, 1968, that the *Texas Observer* "broke" the McCrocklin plagiarism story, but at least two sources indicate the reporting was submitted to the publication up to two years prior. *Observer* editorial staffers said that they had simply wanted to see how the Texas State academic community responded.

When the Texas State University System Board of Regents met in San Antonio on August 20, 1968, the president, Midland attorney Emil C. Rassman, reported that he'd received a letter from Dr. McCrocklin assuring him that McCrocklin's dissertation was his own work. Rassman also stated that an examination of the points made by the *Texas Observer* had been conducted by members of the board and that Rassman was "satisfied that Dr. McCrocklin is blameless." He added, "On behalf of this board, I express complete confidence in the integrity and professional qualities of Dr. McCrocklin." McCrocklin, who was still in Washington, D.C., serving as the undersecretary of Department of Health, Education and Welfare, did not comment. And neither did the *College Star*.

The McCrocklin dissertation debate enjoyed a low profile in the *Star* until September 27, 1968, when editor Terry Collier wrote a front-page piece titled "McCrocklin Paper Reviewed." In it, Collier detailed reporting from the *Observer* piece, the board meeting in San Antonio and a recent *Detroit News* article published by former Marine Corps colonel R.D. Heinl. Heinl revealed that when the Naval Institute originally accepted the McCrocklin dissertation for book treatment, "a Marine historian spotted the similarity between major portions of the manuscript and earlier sources," including Lieutenant Colonel Clyde H. Metcalf's "History of the United States Marine Corps" (1939) and the "Hart Report" (put together by Major Franklin A. Hart), an obscure manuscript that detailed the history of Marine Corps involvement with the Garde d'Haiti (the Haitian gendarmerie). Heinl stated that when the Naval Institute was made aware of the similarities, it agreed to continue publication of the book only if Dr. McCrocklin was listed as the "compiler" rather than the author. When Collier contacted McCrocklin with questions on September 25, 1968, he received a "reserved 'no comment.'"

To the *Star*'s credit, it also ran an important editorial titled "Tell It Like It Is":

> *Before Lyndon B. Johnson became President of these United States, San Marcos and Southwest Texas State College were little known across the nation. But since the President has been in office, SWTexas has ridden on the wings of LBJ's popularity, and his tenure in the White House certainly has not hurt the college.*
>
> *It would seem that with his nearing exit from Washington, SWTexas and the neighboring community would recede into the obscure central Texas setting. Not so.*
>
> *On the contrary, the college is still in the limelight. Reason: the recent controversy over the writings of Dr. James H. McCrocklin, president of the college who is presently serving as undersecretary in the Department of Health, Education and Welfare.*
>
> *Such publications as* Time Magazine, Newsweek, *the* Daily Texan, *the* Detroit News, *the* Texas Observer, *the* Washington

Post *and the Houston and San Antonio papers have printed stories lately on the controversy over Dr. McCrocklin's writings on Marine involvement in the Haitian crisis (1915–1934). The subject has been under intense study for the past two months and has rated front page coverage in some metropolitan dailies.*

According to the published reports, similarities have been discovered between Dr. McCrocklin's dissertation and his wife's thesis and two articles written by Marine Corps officers. The story is long and complicated. Few people actually know all the details, including many presently writing about the situation.

The State Board of Regents recently opened investigations into the matter after having issued a confidence vote in favor of Dr. McCrocklin's "integrity and professional qualifications." Numerous other interests are also in reserve. The one person who can end rumor, establish fact and, at the same time, dispel current false accusations is Dr. McCrocklin himself.

This is not a statement of doubt in the reputation of this college's president. It is a proposal that he clear up the situation with a complete, well-founded explanation, and give up the "no comment" tactic. Not only is his character being questioned, but the college and the students of this institution also are feeling the squeeze.[49]

The *Star* editorial perfectly encapsulated the situation and the pressing issues at hand. The story *was* "long and complicated," and the only party who could "end rumor, establish fact and, at the same time, dispel current false accusations" was McCrocklin himself. By then, however, he'd forgotten what he told the *San Antonio Express* a few years earlier. McCrocklin did not "make decisions quickly" on any aspect of the plagiarism charges, and because of this, he went on to "complicate the situation by delaying." In the immediate short term, it didn't seem to hurt him—just Texas State.

In early September, Johnson appointed McCrocklin to a United States delegation to the United Nations Educational, Scientific and Cultural Organization (UNESCO) conference in Paris on October 15, 1968. On September 25, Oregon senator Wayne Morse, who had rejected the Gulf of Tonkin Resolution, objected to McCrocklin's selection to the delegation due to the controversy surrounding his dissertation and academic standing. On October 2, the U.S. Senate Foreign Relations Committee overrode Morse's objection, and McCrocklin was approved. While McCrocklin was in Paris, however, things at Texas State escalated.

On October 25, 1968, unidentified parties placed yellow, mimeographed, four-paragraph notices that brought attention to McCrocklin's dissertation controversy into an unknown number of copies of the *College Star*. The notices were unsigned, because their originators feared reprisals from the administration. Then, after the scuttlebutt around the campus suggested the student newspaper was being censored, the *Star* actually published an editorial titled "Star Not Censored," but in the "Reader's Pulse" section, John Pfeffer bemoaned the fact that free speech, especially in terms of an open dialogue on McCrocklin's dissertation issue, was being driven underground:

> *Why the fear of freedom of speech, and the freedom of examination, and the right to know how and why our leaders stand on certain issues? Have all channels of open discussion been closed?*

In early November, Nick Thiele, who had earlier addressed the time for action after Martin Luther King's assassination, solicited permission from Dean Martine to stage a demonstration to emphasize the student body's concerns over the questions of professional integrity that had been raised regarding President McCrocklin. "It was hoped that such action would show Dr. McCrocklin that we students would like to hear an explanation

McCrocklin protest in the rain at Texas State on February 20, 1969. *From the 1969 Pedagog yearbook.*

of [the] charges made against him," Thiele communicated at the time, "as we stand to be harmed the most as his reputation suffers and causes that of our school to suffer."

Martine rejected Thiele's request and said that McCrocklin would explain himself when he returned in January. Thiele was not satisfied:

> *If Dr. McCrocklin can explain in January, why can't he do it now? If there is an explanation, one would hope that it is one which doesn't have to be prepared for delivery in January, but one which is real enough to be offered at any time. The dean said the president was in town two weeks ago. Why didn't he explain himself then? It seems that, in the end, we arrive at the question of whether this school is run for the benefit of the administration or for the good of the students.*

On November 15, 1968, a student country-western vocalist (presumably with a guitar) was heard singing a song with the lyrics, "Mama don't allow any plagiarism around here…" on campus. By Thanksgiving break of 1968, McCrocklin's silence was being condemned roundly, and in the "Reader's Pulse" section of the November 22 edition of the *Star*, Bob Gier commented on a campus-wide lapse into unanimity:

> *It has been said that SWT is divided into three parts: the Fraternities, the Independents and the Cowboys. However, these groups appear to be of the same opinion concerning this issue. It's unfortunate that it takes such a controversy to unite the student body, but they're only searching for the truth. One hopes that a student unification will remain after Dr. McCrocklin replies, and the issue is settled.*

If McCrocklin supporters had held out any hope that the academic integrity issue might abate over the long holiday, they were sorely disappointed. On December 6, 1968, a "Reader's Pulse" letter titled "Prexy's Defense Stands on Record" only served to exacerbate matters:

> *During the past few months, we have seen a number of letters to the editor, editorials and articles concerning Dr. McCrocklin's alleged plagiarism in reference to his doctoral dissertation. This is being written in his behalf.*
>
> *In evaluating the man, we should look at what he has done for S.W.T.S.C. [Texas State] since he became president. During his tenure, the growth of the college has been astronomical (4,460 to 8,459). No*

institution can grow this fast without some growing pains and this writer thinks these have been kept to a minimum. Dr. McCrocklin has taken leadership in the state in obtaining faculty benefits such as increases in salaries and the developmental leave. He also has increased the wages of the custodial and maintenance employees. He was one of the first state college presidents to set up the structure making it possible for the faculty and the students to have more voice in the college affairs. He was the first college president to take positive action in making it possible for students to be heard. Examples of this is [sic] *the practice of having the student body president as a member of the Policy Council and student members on the Committee of Fifteen. In addition, he initiated the practice of having breakfast with the student groups in order to listen to their suggestions. These are only a few of his accomplishments in his efforts to upgrade and make S.W.T.S.C. a first-rate college.*

The board of regents have investigated and exonerated Dr. McCrocklin. This should be sufficient. Why then do a few continue to press the question? Better yet, one should also ask why this accusation was made in the first place. Was it done in the name of bettering the college? Or was it done by a few discontented members of the faculty who were trying to "draw blood" because the comfortable little academic nest they had feathered over the years was becoming uncomfortable when they were confronted with having to answer to upgrading themselves? No one, unless they had an ulterior motive would have gone to the trouble of analyzing the documents in such fine detail.[50] *Instead of continuing to harass Dr. McCrocklin on the question, perhaps it would be better for those really interested in this problem to investigate a small minority faculty group who started this and who continue to fan the flame to discover their real reason behind this campaign. This group would like to have the public believe the newspaper which first published the accusation did the "leg work" for the article. A thorough investigation I am certain will reveal otherwise.*

I say, instead of condemning a man accused of something of which he was cleared by the board of regents, look at those who are the accusers and who perhaps are afraid to come out into the open because they themselves could not stand up under investigation.

On December 15, 1968, several Texas State faculty members, who had knowledge of the ongoing controversy and the gumption to challenge the affront lodged by the "Concerned Member of the Faculty," lambasted the "Prexy's Defense" statement in two letters featured in the "Reader's Pulse" section of the *Star*, which were both signed.[51] The first was penned by William A. Emory, a history instructor:

> *I would be tempted to characterize the letter from "A Concerned Member of the Faculty" as irresponsible if it were not so pathetically irrelevant. The issue is not faculty factionalism (even if there were any basis for this particular fantasy) or President McCrocklin's past service to the college. No one doubts that President McCrocklin has contributed much to the growth of this college. The issue, however, is academic dishonesty.*
>
> *There are two essential questions still to be answered. One concerning his role as a member of Mrs. McCrocklin's M.A. thesis committee: (1) Were large portions of President McCrocklin's dissertation taken verbatim or nearly verbatim from a Marine Corps report which was not cited as a source? (2) Are there enough passages that appear verbatim in both President McCrocklin's dissertation and Mrs. McCrocklin's thesis to question the propriety of accepting the thesis as her own work? Perhaps there is no substance to these issues brought forward by several large newspapers and two national magazines, but the irrelevant and anonymous accusations of "A Concerned Member of the Faculty" contribute neither to an understanding of the issues nor to a rational defense of President McCrocklin. Only President McCrocklin can settle this matter.*
>
> *Would "A Concerned Member of the Faculty" accept "service to the college" as an adequate defense against a charge of academic dishonesty leveled at one of his own students? Would that same faculty member feel it would be relevant to the issue for the student to complain that other students had reported his cheating?*

The second letter, penned by government instructor Allan Butcher, was submitted and signed off on by ten members of the faculty and staff, including Dr. Daniel E. Farlow, who would later speak at the October 15 Vietnam Moratorium, Don Graham (English instructor), Patricia Green Harris (English instructor), Mel Jordan (librarian), Steve Marshall (government instructor), Dr. Hal B. Pickle (business instructor),[52] Dr. William C. Pool (history instructor), Robert T. Smith (history instructor) and Walter A. Winsett, who would also later speak at the October 15 Vietnam Moratorium. It read:

> *While last week's letter from "A Concerned Member of the Faculty" is a classic example of fallacious reasoning, and while much of what was*

The "Dirty Dozen."
From left to right and top to bottom: Allan Butcher, Patricia Green Harris, Daniel E. Farlow, Steve Marshall, Robert T. Smith, Hal B. Pickle, William C. Pool, Walter A. Winsett and Don Graham. Mel Jordan and William A. Emory are not pictured.
Courtesy of the Pedagog *yearbooks.*

listed we accept as being correct and a credit to President McCrocklin, these matters are no more relevant to the issue of plagiarism than is the length of his hair or the color of his socks.

There is one aspect of last week's letter with which we concur. We, too, call for a completely free and open investigation as the only way to put to final rest these rumors and gossip. To this end, therefore, we would like to see both students and faculty attend a forum next Tuesday, December 17, at 2:30 p.m. in the Student Center ballroom. The documents in question will be available for examination and discussion. We too are "concerned members of the faculty."

When the *Texas Observer* later reported on the December 17 Texas State gathering to examine the absent president's dissertation, it noted that none of the ten signatories to the second letter had been any of the individuals who originally "alerted" the publication to the suspicious nature of the McCrocklin papers—the "informants" had since departed Texas State. The *Observer*'s December 27 article, "A Forum on McCrocklin," set up the issue at hand halfway through the lead paragraph:

> *Defenders of Dr. McCrocklin, now an undersecretary in the U.S. Department of Health, Education and Welfare, insist the charges of plagiarism are the vicious slander of a group of malcontents. The attackers believe that they have evidence of a serious case of academic dishonesty and that to ignore the issue would destroy the integrity of the institution.*

On the afternoon of December 17, 1968, the overflow crowd at the Student Center ballroom spilled into every adjacent space. Retired Marine Corps colonel R.D. Heinl even showed up to report on the forum for the *Detroit News.* Just before the event commenced, however, the dean of the college, Dr. Joe H. Wilson, emerged and read a statement sent along by the acting Texas State president, Dr. Leland Derrick. Derrick's message characterized the meeting as "ill-timed" and asked the participants to postpone it.

> *I cannot believe that after serious reflection any person moved by a sense of justice would try to accuse a man in absentia.....Nothing can be gained by trying the matters at issue in this forum; nothing can be lost by postponing action until Dr. McCrocklin's return in January.*

Then, an unidentified male member of the administration stood up, his voice "shaking with emotion," and said, "You have been patient for several months, why not one more month?"

The forum, chaired by English instructor Ben Archer, was held as planned, and the situation was tense. The participating students were frustrated; the participating faculty and staff were concerned about the security of their jobs and the future of the institution. Football players were reportedly sent to "shout down" any anti-McCrocklin dialogue, and some individuals—including one off-duty police officer—were sent there to spy on the proceedings for the administration.[53] "There were a lot of scared people," Archer told the *Hillside Scene* in 1990. "You didn't know who your friends were and people were very nervous about expressing themselves in public." One student called the forum-staging faculty members "bigoted

Texas State students participating in the McCrocklin protest on February 20, 1969. *From the spring 1990 issue of the* Hillside Scene *student magazine.*

ax-grinders," while another student lauded them, remarking that they had shown real courage and integrity by "insisting that they [would] not stand for plagiarism within their own ranks."

The faculty members who staged the forum had reproduced pages of Dr. McCrocklin's dissertation and Mrs. McCrocklin's thesis and placed them side-by-side on separate overhead projection screens. Participants from the audience called out page numbers at random, and the overhead projector operators matched the pages up. Some pages were identical and some only differentiated by two or three words. After the first several pages were examined, Heinl reported that "no one wanted anymore." A sickening unrest settled into the breasts of many witnesses of the comparisons, but the forum went on. Participants were moved to Evans Auditorium after the allotted time in the Student Center ballroom had ended, and after that, they moved to the local Holiday Inn. Heinl remained throughout, sharing the background of the original Marine reports that McCrocklin had copied for his dissertation, and he clearly demonstrated that the college president's plagiarism had been as bad as his wife's.

Unfortunately, however, even though the process had exposed McCrocklin's academic dishonesty and cast Texas State in a shabby light, many still supported the president, despite his sins, and clung to their faith in him, regardless of the facts. "There were people in the community that were told that this was a Communist plot," Farlow said. "There were at least three different kinds of plots identified for being responsible for the whole thing."

8

DISSECTING TIME

Doc carries an empty ten-cent package of green-bean seeds in the elastic band
that holds the camouflage cover on his helmet. Others draw elaborate calendars.
Defining time, detailing and dissecting time (Each goes home after his 365 days
in country.). Time is life. LOVE and PEACE stretch around some helmets. There is
F.T.A. (Fuck the Army)—STONE MAN—LOVE BABY—KID KILL.
They wear and carry Montagnard bracelets,[54] peace symbols, headbands,
rabbit's feet, the queen of hearts, the ace of spades, bibles, pictures of Jesus and
the Pope, Buddhist medals blessed by monks, pictures of girlfriends and wives; all
amulets worn to keep the dark off, to keep arms, legs and balls from flying away.
No, Billy Graham[55] is not considered protection. Jimi Hendrix is.
—David Bayless, "A Little in Love," Austin Chronicle, *June 25, 1993*

By 1969, the debate about the antiwar movement, peace protests and the so-called hippies at Texas State was well underway. In a letter to the editor in the January 31, 1969 edition of the *College Star*, Texas State student Jerry Robinson complained about the way hippies dressed and called them the "moral cowards" of the generation. He blamed their attitudes on higher education: "They are victims, in effect, of learned people who stand in college-school classrooms and go too far in the probing of young minds. These learned people lead young people to question their present history and future."

A couple of students responded to Robinson's letter in the *Star* on February 7, but the most interesting response came from the *Star* Editorial Department itself on February 21:

Now that SWT has arrived on the "big-time" college scene, complete with a boycott[56] and sit-in,[57] there are some factions that have been and will continue to grumble that the college is undoubtedly going to the dogs, or at least to the hippies.

They will contend that the ominous, brooding mass of ne'er-do-wells who do nothing but incite trouble are sending the country and this college down the road to "rack and ruin" by their constantly negative protests.

In short, they conclude, when one considers student unrest, the problems of poverty, the cities, Vietnam, the entire scene seems to be in disorder.

But disorder is not necessarily bad. For years, this campus and the average citizen have been complacent and, frankly, smug when it came to the state of affairs on the campus or throughout the nation. They were confident in the belief that any problem would work itself out; success was simply the American way. Still, the problems kept rearing their heads.

The result in the nation has been disillusionment and reevaluation of what is to be faced and what is to be done. The right to question is at hand, a simplistic glossing over solves nothing. By realistically assessing what is to be done, by criticizing, there can be a workable solution to the problems to be faced.

The country seems to finally be coming to squarely view the contradictions, perplexities and hypocrisies in our society. The college, too, must maturely face criticism and view with healthy respect the negative and positive arguments.

It is imperative that an institution realize that protesters and dissenters may also have the good of the school as their motive. And if they do, then the two have common ground from which to work. And the problems can be solved.

The editorial was insightful and challenging but also optimistic. It stressed the opportunity for unity.

The December 17, 1968 forum had been damning for McCrocklin and the school, and students and faculty expected some sort of resolution or closure, a way to move forward, when the Texas State president returned from Washington, D.C., on January 21. It didn't come. McCrocklin simply carried on. He did not respond to the charges of plagiarism or defend himself. A decision regarding McCrocklin's reelection to the Texas State presidency by the Board of Regents was scheduled for February 21, 1969. McCrocklin announced that he would explain the alleged similarities between his doctoral dissertation and his wife's master's thesis following a faculty meeting on February 24, a date that fell safely after his contract extension.

On February 20, approximately 250 Texas State students stood with signs and umbrellas in the cold, drizzling rain in front of Flowers Hall to protest McCrocklin's rehiring. Their placards said things like "Don't Sell the Reputation of SWT" and "NO COMMENT, *please*. NO CONTRACT!" Though the demonstration was not staged at the student handbook–designated "student expression" location or within the standard, handbook-allotted hours, the organizer of the protest, John Pfeffer, had solicited and received permission for the demonstration from Dean Martine. Martine was present at the event and at one point even held his umbrella over a couple of protesters handing out flyers so they wouldn't get wet. The demonstration lasted from noon to 2:00 p.m.—well past the hours permitted for "Student Expression"—and future San Marcos 10 protesters Paul Cates, Murray Rosenwasser and Sallie Ann Satagaj were all present.

On February 24, 1969, McCrocklin gave a four-page reply to his critics, announcing that he had given his wife permission to use parts of his thesis because, as a civilian, she did not have access to the pertinent documents. He also noted that he wasn't originally a member of her thesis committee but had to fill in after the retirement of a fellow faculty member. As for the plagiarism of the *Hart Report* that he had committed himself, McCrocklin claimed "a number of people wanted the facts of the *Hart Report* made public without damaging [the United States'] relations with Haiti" and he simply obliged them, procuring permission from Lieutenant General Hart (whom McCrocklin implied he served under) and granting all rights and royalties to the U.S. Marine Corps. Most of the rank and file members of the administration, faculty and student government gave McCrocklin a standing ovation for his "good soldier" routine, and for a moment, it appeared as if he might weather the damning facts and the controversy. The Student Senate acknowledged McCrocklin's defense of his dissertation and circulated a petition requesting a commendation of the embattled president "for his past achievements" at the college.

Allan Butcher, however, was quick to point out that though McCrocklin did cite his use of the *Hart Report*, he did so two years after completing his dissertation. Former Texas State student James Green, who was then pursuing a doctorate at the University of Texas and had helped prepare a comparison of the *Hart Report* and the McCrocklin dissertation for the American Association of University Professors, pointed out that McCrocklin's comments suggested that he had played a role in writing the *Hart Report*—but that was impossible. "At the time the report was written," Green observed, "Dr. McCrocklin wasn't even a teenager." Pfeffer said the statement featured a series of "misleading half-truths." When questioned on February 25, Butcher told reporters it was a "safe assumption" that several professors would leave if Texas State retained its current president and that he had been told not to discuss the McCrocklin matter in his classes. He also noted that he was working on his own dissertation at the time. "What I ought to do," Butcher said, "is get a government document and tear off the cover sheet."

The University of Texas—where McCrocklin completed his doctoral work—subsequently announced that it was creating a five-member committee of graduate professors to investigate McCrocklin's dissertation.

In the February 28, 1969 edition of the *College Star*, contributors to the "Reader's Pulse" bandied back and forth about the McCrocklin issue. Texas State student John S. Odell charged that the sleight-of-hand tactics McCrocklin employed in his statement were "an affront to the academic community." Texas State student Lydia Oldham submitted an *ad hominem*[58] pro-McCrocklin observation:

> *The terms "student leaders" and "intellectuals" have been applied to the wrong people by several newspapers. This "trouble" was caused by a minority group who are mentally competent but are not sufficiently mature to be able to judge others in such matters.*
>
> *The majority of the protesting group who are against Dr. McCrocklin either are jealous or don't know what they're protesting; they are merely propaganda, "band-wagon" riders who do not sufficiently know the issues.*

The heavy hitter among these letters, however, was written by Don Graham, one of the signatories of the Butcher letter that announced the forum:

> *Mr. McCrocklin's statement, however satisfactory to faculty sycophants, is unacceptable to anybody who has examined the document in question—his dissertation, her thesis* [Mrs. McCrocklin's master's thesis] *and the seminal father of both, the* Hart Report. *The key point in McCrocklin's statement, I take it, is that he had Hart's permission to use the* Hart Report. *Splendid, except that the permission to use is hardly the permission to duplicate, which is what McCrocklin did....Around town, Mr. McCrocklin is known as Xerox, the perfect copier. He has given us no grounds for thinking otherwise.*

Texas State students participating in the McCrocklin protest on February 20, 1969. *From the spring 1990 issue of the* Hillside Scene *student magazine.*

In early April, the *Star* reported that students involved in the initial McCrocklin protest in February were planning a second demonstration in early May, before McCrocklin would present his case to the University of Texas.

A second protest was unnecessary. McCrocklin resigned on April 19, 1969.

Still defiant, McCrocklin claimed he was having difficulty in rounding up the documents he needed to exonerate himself. He said that he had come to the regrettable conclusion that he must step down for the good of the college and so he might devote his full time and effort to "dispelling the false smear upon [his] personal integrity, the quality of a degree from the

University of Texas" and upon Texas State. There is no evidence he ever pursued these goals.

Many who remained at Texas State after the McCrocklin debacle continued to entertain various levels of confusion and denial about the fiasco for years, but the historical record is less equivocal. By the early 1980s, McCrocklin was already figuring into studies of academic dishonesty, including *Betrayers of Truth: Fraud and Deceit in the Halls of Science* (1982):

> *The piles of papers, books and articles that have mushroomed in the years following the Second World War have concealed dozens of plagiarists.... Many of these cases of piracy would have gone unreported except that the principals later in their careers achieved positions of power and repute that resulted in widespread and detailed examination of their record. A case in point is that of James H. McCrocklin, who, when charges emerged in 1968, was president of Southwest Texas College. A magazine in Texas revealed that his Ph.D. and his wife's master's thesis were strikingly alike, and that both had borrowed heavily from an old, obscure Marine Corps report. What was at first merely a personal embarrassment quickly became a public controversy. McCrocklin denied any wrongdoing, and public opinion held that he might outlast the charges, especially since McCrocklin was a personal friend of then President Lyndon B. Johnson, and Southwest Texas State College was Johnson's alma mater. Nonetheless, McCrocklin resigned his post in April 1969.*

Betrayers of Truth also makes some important ancillary points. Most plagiarism involves obscure manuscripts, and the obscurity of the *Hart Report* made it difficult to track down and access. It's almost impossible to imagine that this factor didn't enter into McCrocklin's initial thought process when he willfully and knowingly committed plagiarism. Still more troubling, however, is the number of Texas State faculty and staff members who willfully and knowingly ignored the facts of the matter going forward.

———◆———

After McCrocklin's resignation, Leland Derrick resumed his role as acting president, and the transition administration proceeded to handle dissent in much the same way that the McCrocklin administration had. The newspaper coverage indicated that four faculty members who were active in the McCrocklin controversy (three of whom had signed the letter calling for the December 17, 1968 McCrocklin forum) received one-year terminal contracts. These faculty members included Butcher, who had been with the college for six years; Steve Marshall, who had been with the college for two years; Dr. Robert Smith,[59] who had been at the school for three years; and Dr. Y.K. Malik, an assistant professor of government. In mid-May 1969, acting Texas State president Derrick admitted that two of the aforelisted four faculty members had been dismissed because of their involvement in the McCrocklin ordeal. Derrick said, "We felt these fellows didn't act in the best interest of the college by going outside the structure of the faculty on some matters." When pressed on the term "faculty structure," Derrick continued. "We have a faculty senate. They can follow the normal procedures by going through the senate."

Butcher was obviously dismissed for his role in the McCrocklin ordeal as well, but Derrick chalked up his termination—like that of John Quincy Adams years before—to his inability to finish his doctoral work. Butcher was slated to receive his PhD from the University of Texas in a few months.

An immigrant from India, Dr. Malik had authored six books and was in the process of completing his seventh, which was to be published by the Institute of Race Relations in London, England. He was also scheduled to present a paper to the American Political Science Association in New York City that coming September—making him the first Texas State professor ever approached to address the group.

Patricia Green Harris and Don Graham left of their own accord. Harris went to Texas A&M University, where she received a PhD in applied linguistics in 1982. She spent most of the rest of her academic career with the English Language Institute at Texas A&M, teaching English as a second language.[60]

Graham left Texas State before he could be fired and went on to become an accomplished Texas author and University of Texas scholar.[61] "I was young and kind of a firebrand at the time," Graham remembered. "I became pretty outspoken and that letter I wrote to the *Star* really angered the chairman of my department." During the spring semester of 1968, with *Hays County Free Press* publisher Bob Barton's backing (the same Bob Barton who would later de-esculate tempers at the October 15, 1969 Vietnam Moratorium), Graham ran for the office of Hays County Democratic chairmanship. He didn't win, but it was a memorable campaign. "I had just passed my oral PhD exams at UT, and I was feeling pretty fine," Graham said. "I even had cards and bumper

Texas State students participating in a study-in, protesting the "political purge" of four instructors involved in the McCrocklin "defrocking." *From the 1969* Pedagog *yearbook.*

stickers printed up." His campaign slogan was a classic: *Vote for Graham. He ain't no cracker.*

English instructor Walter A. Winsett also left Texas State due to a terminal contract, but it didn't make the news. He subsequently applied for another position as a college instructor but was informed he was being blackballed by Texas State administrators. He went on to work for All-Church Press in Fort Worth before accepting a position at the Denton Public Library, where he remained until 2004. Winsett passed away on June 6, 2015, but his wife, Stella, remembers the McCrocklin controversy and the Texas State administration's stance on progressives:

> *At one point, Bob Walts* [the chairman of the English Department] *actually told Walter that he needed to get control of me....I was working for Bob Barton at the Colloquium Bookstore. Bob ran the Hays County Democratic coalition, and at one point, he got me to run for precinct chair. They told Walter that I needed to stay away from Barton. And, of course, we ignored them.*[62]

Many Texas State students did not respond to the administration's house-cleaning measures favorably. They began boycotting classes and blaming their absences on the "McCrocklin flu." They also started petitions criticizing the professor removals. In one petition, they condemned what they perceived to be a "political purge" and warned that such a blatant assault on academic freedom and integrity would diminish the value of their degrees and endanger "the free atmosphere that is necessary at a college or university."

On Wednesday, May 21, 1969, approximately fifty students—including Paul Cates and Sallie Ann Satagaj—participated in a "study-in" on the Quad between Flowers Hall and the Science Building to protest the firings. The participants sat peacefully and quietly, and some held signs. One sign read, "Fire Fascist Administrators—Not Intelligent Professors." A few demonstrators brandished bubble wands, and soon, the warm spring air was full of bubbles. One elderly professor passing by told reporters that "Lawrence Welk would go out of his gourd if he saw this."[63]

Texas State instructor Steve Dibrell heard about the protest while he was having lunch at home and rushed back up to the campus to "say a few words in [*sic*] behalf of the administration":

> *I'm just sick and tired of all this upheaval on campus, and I feel it's about time some of the faculty acts like faculty and takes some responsibility. This all goes back to the McCrocklin affair, which I call a modern-day lynching. That whole thing was planned to undermine and destroy confidence in leadership—leadership of our campus and our country, too, since I think it was originally started to cast a bad light on former President Johnson.*

One administration official, who insisted he remain anonymous, also shared his thoughts: "Thank God this is the last week [of the spring semester]. I'm fed up here with hippies, long-hairs, beads and beards. Talk about freedom of expression and academic freedom—I'm ready for a little freedom for the administration."

A local TV station covered the protest, but most of the newspaper reporting simply focused on the demonstration's small numbers to downplay it. The coverage failed to mention that the semester was ending, which meant fewer students were around anyway. Some media outlets noted that, despite the fact that the demonstration was conducted in an orderly manner, it was still technically against the "student expression" rules; but Dean Martine never showed up, and no one gave the protesters three minutes to disperse or face suspension.

After a jarring semester and cramming for finals, the Texas State class of 1969 received their diplomas late. Southwest Texas State College became Southwest Texas State University in the spring semester of 1969, and the school was waiting on documents with the new university name engraved across the top. In the end, the name change was just one more accomplishment—or consequence—of James H. McCrocklin's tenure.

On October 31, 1969, McCrocklin's PhD was declared "null, void and of no effect" at the University of Texas, and the University's Board of Regents voted to no longer recognize McCrocklin's doctoral degree. After his resignation, McCrocklin still had friends in high places and bought a real estate firm that became one of the most successful in central Texas. McCrocklin was interviewed by the Texas State *Hillside Scene* magazine in 1990, and though he didn't have much to say about stepping down as the president of the university, he also didn't harbor any ill will. In fact, in 1988, he donated a valuable collection of pre-Columbian artifacts to the school.

9
REINSTATEMENT

It is dangerous to be right when the government is wrong.
—Voltaire

In the late 1960s, it had become a custom for the Texas State Art Department to place new paintings by student artists on the walls of the Old Main administration building. In April 1969, one of the paintings placed on display featured a Vietnam War theme. The work, by Roger Rietz, was quickly condemned and ordered to be taken down by the dean of the School of Liberal Arts, Ralph H. Houston. The Art Department promptly removed the artwork and put up a new one. Rietz's painting was relocated to the wall of a less-trafficked hall in the Art Department offices.

Several Texas State students took notice, including Juan R. Palomo. In a letter to the "Reader's Pulse" section of the *College Star*, Palomo accused Texas State administrators of engaging in behavior unfit for a proper university. He pointedly argued that removing the artwork of a student because of its political leanings suggested that the school was a "second-rate" institution that had no business aspiring to the title of a full-fledged university.

Six months later, after the first Texas State Vietnam Moratorium, critics of the local antiwar movement came out of the woodwork, but the *College Star* took a bold stand in its main editorial on October 17, 1969. The title of the piece was "Moratoriums Should Continue":

> *They came from all sections of the campus on Wednesday—longhairs and shorthairs, Greeks and independents, freshmen just out of high school and*

service veterans. But they were all there for one reason—to protest a war they considered contradictory to American ideals.

They weren't there to make trouble or to support the V.C. [Viet Cong] as some critics tried to misrepresent it. Instead they came to express what campus Catholic chaplain Reverend Charles Gielow labeled "their deep weariness with the never, never-ending bloodshed."

And they stayed, despite official pressure and unofficial threats.

The hecklers were there, making caustic comments and shouting obscenities. But the demonstrators never lowered themselves to their raucous critics' level.

Instead, they talked quietly among themselves or sang folk songs. Rather than feeling antagonism towards their critics, the feelings were more those of pity that the hecklers couldn't share in the sense of unity and brotherhood that filled the crisp autumn air.

Even when the campus security forces were withdrawn and there was fear that the hecklers might attempt violent disruption, the demonstrators stayed....The nationwide moratorium will be expanded to two days in November, three in December and so on until the war ends.

President Nixon has stated that the moratorium will have no effect on his policy making. But, when the voice of the American people cries out as it did [Thursday], then only a deaf man can ignore it, a man oblivious to the needs of his nation.

A photo of the Roger Rietz painting that was removed from a hallway in the Old Main administration building. *From the 1969* Pedagog *yearbook.*

Such events cannot help but have an effect on the feelings of a reasonable leader. And President Nixon has shown himself to be a reasonable leader.

For that reason, the moratoriums should continue, continue until no man can any longer deny that the American people are tired of war.

The negative responses to this *Star* opinion were swift and frenzied. The Student Senate passed a resolution requesting that the Publications Committee investigate the *Star* for "causing" student unrest on campus. Just four days after former president James McCrocklin's PhD was nullified by the University of Texas's Board of Regents, student senator Dave Bowman straight-facedly suggested that the *Star* was creating "a general feeling of unrest and distrust." Associated Students president Bill Miller added that a number of students had complained to him that the *Star* was biased, including some members of the *Star* staff. But an unidentified Texas State professor—anonymous presumably because they had been at the school long enough to be familiar with the administration's tactics—put their proverbial foot down in the "Reader's Pulse" section of the November 7, 1969 edition of the *Star*:

I wish to congratulate you for your editorial of October 31 in the College Star *concerning the administration's sanctions against participants in the October 15 Moratorium. What is involved here is much more than the pros and cons of U.S. withdrawal from Vietnam; it is the right of citizens to criticize their government and take action on behalf of their interests. The moratorium was an orderly and peaceful event, supported not by extremists but many concerned citizens who are usually considered as decent and patriotic even by compulsive conservatives.*

Yet, the actions taken by the University's administration against participants in the moratorium resemble those normally applied to spies and Mafia; they are actions typically associated with people like Hitler, Stalin and Joseph McCarthy. It was not enough for the administration to seek information about participants; even worse, they forced students to inform on their peers and instructors. A proctor who refused to solicit denunciations from freshmen in his dormitory was fired. Denounced faculty members were reprimanded by administrators for "violating the right of students to attend classes."[64] I did not know students were so keen on attendance.

These dubious tactics create a general atmosphere of distrust and suspicion on the campus, leaving a situation of constant secret warfare of everybody against everybody. The principle of divide et impera[65] *has worked well for the administration in the past, arousing students against students, faculty against faculty, and students against faculty. But it is time to recognize that the real dividing line is between students and faculty on the one hand and the administration on the other....The issue at stake here is academic freedom and the right to execute one's civic responsibilities. Those who take everything for granted and suppress the expression of doubt (the essence of all philosophical and scientific endeavors) have no place at a university.*

The stark missive concluded with the obvious statement: "I hope you understand that it would not be advisable for me to disclose my identity."

It's hard to gauge the blast radius of this startling articulation. The writer was bold but anonymous; the current *Star* editor, Steve Blackmon, was brave for publishing it, and it would cost him the editorship.

The Texas State administration had exhibited pro-war leanings well before the October 15 Moratorium, and that demonstration had been

The San Marcos 10 being cordoned off by campus security and "jocks" at the November 13, 1969 Vietnam Moratorium sit-in. *Courtesy of the University Archives, Texas State University.*

popular and successful in a way that raised the current officialdom's hackles. Now, the student newspaper was lauding protest in general, and faculty members were calling out the administration, how it governed and what it deemed should be done to control the campus. Regardless of motive, Texas State officials decided to obstruct the November protest by reducing its visibility as much as possible. Martine spoke with the November 13 demonstration planners after the October 15 event and restricted the protest to a designated "free speech area" in front of the Old Main building, away from the central Quad. He also issued restrictive demonstration and assembly time requirements.

This was a far cry from what had been done in terms of recent protests, and the November 13 demonstration organizers felt they were being treated unfairly and that their First Amendment rights were being infringed upon. Before the November 13 Moratorium, protest organizers spoke with two attorneys recommended by the American Civil Liberties Union (ACLU) to determine their rights.[66] They concluded that they had a First Amendment right to hold another protest in the original location as long as they didn't block Quad traffic or create a disturbance. Dean Martine and the university disagreed.

On the evening of Monday, November 3, 1969, President Nixon delivered an address to the nation that reportedly reached seventy million Americans (over one-third of the U.S. population at the time and possibly two-thirds of the voting population). The October 15 Vietnam Moratorium had been surprisingly successful, and Nixon wanted to regain momentum and gin up support for the war. The following excerpt from Evan Thomas's book, *Being Nixon: A Man Divided* (2015), is instructive:

> [Nixon] *pledged to "win the peace," using the same gauzy, if uplifting, phrase he had employed during his presidential campaign. He said that he had a "plan for peace," although he did not spell out what it was, beyond more fighting and talking, coupled with gradual troop withdrawals....Then he began his peroration:*
>
> *"And so tonight—to you, the great silent majority of my fellow Americans—I ask or your support....Let us be united for peace. Let*

us also be united against defeat. Because let us understand: North Vietnam cannot defeat or humiliate the United States. Only Americans can do that."

…"Silent majority" was an old phrase meaning dead people, noted Nixon wordsmith William Safire—to join the silent majority meant to die and go to a cemetery. But Nixon's brilliant reinvention of the term was a political masterstroke. It was a natural extension of a theme he had been working on.…He had long spoken of "quiet Americans" and "forgotten Americans"; now he had a way to capture the flag back from the protesters—the "loud minority" who, alone, could humiliate the United States.

Nixon's address struck a cord with conservative, pro-war elements in the Texas State Student Senate. They, like the Nixon administration, were convinced that the silent majority supported the war and resented the antiwar protests, so they passed legislation sponsoring a student referendum on the matter and scheduled the referendum for November 18, five days after the upcoming moratorium.

On November 13, the day of the demonstration at Texas State, U.S. representative William Jennings Bryan Dorn said the national moratorium movement was an attempt to reduce President Nixon "to a cringing vassal and a stooge of mobs and demonstrators." Republican senator Charles E. Goodell of New York said, "It does not service the cause of peace to indulge in inflammatory rhetoric that can only deepen the division in this country." Goodell's fellow Republican senator Strom Thurmond of South Carolina claimed that even sincere protesters were "part of the international Communist movement." And syndicated columnist Thurman Sensing, whose work appeared in several rural newspapers around Texas, charged: "The organizers of the protests have duped thousands of people into participating in what is fundamentally a communist political operation designed to crack the will of the American government and people."

———◆———

After the San Marcos 10 were suspended, Annie Burleson went to her dorm to call her dad. "I thought he was going to be *so* proud of me," Burleson said. "He had taught me to stand up for myself.…He was not exactly thrilled that that I got kicked out of school," Burleson remembered. "But he still supported me." Meanwhile, Al Henson went on the run. "We had to leave the campus immediately," Henson recalled. "Within twenty-four hours. I didn't tell my parents, but the university called them that afternoon. I had some friends who had a house in Wimberley. They told me I could come and stay there. I couldn't face my dad's disappointment. I was basically running scared."

On the evening of the San Marcos 10's suspension, hundreds of their classmates, and no small number of faculty members, marched on what was to become the new administration building (down the hill from the Old Main building) to protest the 10's treatment. Dean Martine made an appearance and was jeered all around. Kent Garrett wound up speaking at the protest because members of the San Marcos 10 had been banned from campus. Burleson, however, had snuck back to attend the rally. She and her boyfriend, Tony Sisto—who worked in the library that was already open in the new administration building—took an elevator to the balcony of the library and looked out over the demonstrators. "It was amazing," Burleson said. "Here were all these students, some of whom I'm sure had helped rope us off earlier in the day. But now they were a part of this whole other group, gathered there to protest what happened. Even if they didn't agree with us, they thought we had been treated harshly and unfairly. It was very gratifying." Burleson and Sisto were stopped by a security guard on the way out, and Sisto was almost kicked out of school. "They made me move back on campus instead," said Sisto. "But I just paid for the dorm room and never stayed in it."

The next morning, throngs of protesting students reappeared, and in a prepared statement, James B. Hobbs—now assistant to the new president, Billy Mac Jones—did his best bad cop impression to Jones's good cop. "Disruption and disorder hold no place at Southwest Texas State University," he proclaimed melodramatically. President Jones later told a group of student representatives that it wasn't the university's intent to hurt anyone. "After all," Jones said, "we are here for the same purpose—education." Hobbs added, "We want to speed this whole matter up as much as possible, so that we can get into the courts and get a clear-cut decision."

Henson bumped into some of his friends from high school a day or two later, and they told him his parents were trying to reach him. He reluctantly called home. "I was very afraid," Henson recalled. "I remember having an argument with my dad about long hair in high school. It was a generational argument that was probably happening in many households. After the suspension, it was like, 'Oh my God. That money for college went down the drain. He's gonna be so angry.'" Henson's dad surprised him. "There was no

Dean Floyd Martine questioning instructor Allan Black at the November 13, 1969 Vietnam Moratorium. *Courtesy of the University Archives, Texas State University.*

shouting," he remembered. "My dad said, 'I don't necessarily agree with your stand on the war, but I've got to tell you—if this is something you really believe in, I could not be any prouder of you for standing up for your rights.'"

"It was an amazing relief," Henson added. "It gave me fodder for a whole other level of love and respect for my dad."

Cates's parents responded differently. "They were very unhappy," he recalled. "My father was an army officer and they were not pleased. They cut me off financially."

After their suspension, several members of the San Marcos 10 met with lawyers and instituted procedures to file a grievance. Then, they began fighting their dismissal through channels at the school, and their first step was to present their case to the Student-Faculty Review Board.

In the meantime, the November 14, 1969 edition of the *Star* covered the reaction to the suspensions. The editorial cartoon, provided by Kent Garrett, featured a cowboy pondering, "I just cain't understand why them dad blamed hippies git all dooded up in them wierd [*sic*] bohemian clothes. Why cain't they dress like us AmeriKKKans?"

The main editorial, titled "Sad Day in Mudville," took the middle ground:

> *To Borrow a phrase from Grantland Rice's immortal poem, "It's a Sad Day in Mudville." Only that Mudville is Southwest Texas State University. And there is not just one Mighty Casey that has struck out, but the entire university.*
>
> *The events of yesterday can only leave one with a sour taste in his mouth, and whether either side is in the right is not really the question. The university is at stake and we've just burned it.…This university needs the young, probing minds of these Americans, for too many people are more willing to sit quietly and let things go.*
>
> *People always applaud crusaders and these people are truly crusaders. They believe in what they are doing. How many people do you know that really do something about something in which they believe? Whether you agree with what they are doing is, again, not the question. At least they are doing something. But, now, these people are lost to the university. And this, also, is not healthy for the school.*

The most compelling aspect of this "middle ground" editorial is its reference to the San Marcos 10 as "crusaders." Crusaders of what? Crusaders for what?

The minute Martine appeared at the November 13 demonstration to threaten the fifty or so students who had gathered in silent protest, most of them immediately departed. Martine then left, allowing the pro-war onlookers to demean and intimidate anyone who remained. Why did Martine leave? What was Martine's intent in leaving? Did he want the pro-war contingent to threaten the protesters? If so, that's exactly what they did, and that is, again, why instructor Allan Black stepped under the ropes to stand with the demonstrators.

The demonstration had been peaceful and largely silent at that point; it was the pro-war antagonists who were causing a scene. At the October 15 Moratorium, Martine had actually mollified the overzealous, pro-war crowd. If he had remained at the November 13 event, would the demonstration have even developed into a spectacle that could be characterized as disruptive? The question of who the real instigators were at the November 13 Moratorium has never been sufficiently answered; this issue will be explored later, but it was arguably not the "crusaders," who, while sitting quietly in the grass, were hardly crusading.

Paul Cates was a former student senator. David Bayless was a former baseball letterman at Texas State who'd served in Vietnam. Sallie Ann Satagaj was enrolled in the college honors program. Annie Burleson was a member of the *College Star* staff. Joe Saranello was a campus leader and "sharp as a tack," said Cates. McConchie was a former college football player at Texas A&M and was a husband and father. Vykoukal was an education major. Murray Rosenwasser had also served in the military and returned home to take care of his ailing father. The "Sad Day in Mudville" editorial didn't characterize members of the San Marcos 10 as hippies or troublemakers because they weren't. They were good students. They were intelligent and informed.

In the original gathering, the 10 were joined by dozens of other intelligent, informed classmates, including Gaillardian Terry McCabe, Kent Garrett, Juan R. Palomo and Tony Sisto, but these individuals took their leave upon the threat of suspension. "Opposing the war was bigger than occupying that particular piece of real estate at the time," McCabe said. "I only had one semester left," said Palomo. "I wanted to finish school. I had a low draft number and I did not want to go to Vietnam." Sisto was also concerned with his vulnerability to the draft in the event that he was kicked out. Garrett had actually headed to the Student Center just before Martine arrived to grab some Cokes, and by the time he returned, the 10 had already been cordoned off.

Most left, but ten remained.

Why?

———•———

David O. McConchie and Frances Vykoukal are gone now. McConchie lost a long battle with a degenerative brain disease in New Mexico on September 9, 2003. "David was a pacifist until he wasn't," said McConchie's ex-wife, Sherry Ligarde. "When the dean came around and told them they had to leave, that was it. David dug his heels in."

Vykoukal succumbed to cancer on Tuesday, September 28, 2010. Holman and Rosenwasser were by her side. Vykoukal's sisters, Ellen Ermis and Marilyn Svec, said Frances had known the war was not right and that remaining seated at the November 13, 1969 Moratorium demonstration had been practically sacrosanct to her. "It helped shape who she was," said Ermis, who also attended Texas State and worked for the university for several years afterward.

After her graduation from Texas State, Frances attended the San Francisco Art Institute and later received an art education degree at the University of Texas. She taught art at the elementary school level on a Navajo reservation in Utah for years before coming back to Texas to teach in Goliad. Her paintings can still be found in schools and churches in south Texas.

Participating in the demonstration was a matter of principle for Mike Holman. "The war was wrong," he said. "The school was wrong. There was no reason we should have been denied our rights."

"We had gone to a protest in Houston," Sallie Ann Satagaj remembered. "We kept saying, 'What can we do? What can we do?' Then, the national moratoriums started. And we had one."

"There was a war going on," Satagaj said. "People were dying. It was the only thing I knew to do to help stop the war. There was no hesitation at all. I was going to stay, and my action was one of many. And all of these actions together helped bring about a different consciousness."

Rosenwasser and David McConchie participating in the Texas State Vietnam Moratorium on November 13, 1969. *Courtesy of the University Archives, Texas State University.*

"We felt we had a right to stay," Joe Saranello said. "We didn't know how it would ultimately play out—one never does—but we were willing to take a chance, because we knew it was the right thing to do."

As a veteran of the war, Bayless had a slightly different view of the protest. "When I was in Vietnam," said Bayless, "I didn't think it was a bad decision to be there. I had no political sense of things. I thought politics was a black hole, and I didn't care about any of it. But people were dying. You drink a beer with a guy in base camp, and, then, the next day, he's dead.[67] And after a while you start to think."

Bayless thought a lot. "There was no question the war was a lie from the beginning," he said. "From the Gulf of Tonkin to the end, when Nixon said 'peace with honor.' Lies in between, lies throughout. One basket of lies from the beginning to the end."

———◆———

The day after the demonstration, Texas State's administration issued a "Statement to the Faculty of Southwest Texas State University," which read:

> *You, as the faculty of this institution, have the right to know the facts in this situation which occurred yesterday resulting in the suspension of ten students until the Fall Semester, 1970.*
>
> *Their suspension came when they failed to comply with stated University policy. On page 70 of the SWT student handbook, Hill Hints, the following guidelines are published:*
>
> *STUDENT EXPRESSION AREA*
> *Students and University personnel may use the Student Expression Area located on the grass terraces in front of Old Main between the hours of 12 noon to 1 p.m. and from 5 to 7 p.m. Reservations for the Student Expression Area are made through the Dean of Students Office and must be made at least 48 hours in advance.*
>
> *Rules to be observed by users of the area include:*
>
> - *No interference with the free flow of traffic.*
> - *No interruption of the orderly conduct of University affairs.*

- *No obscene materials.*
- *Person making the reservation is responsible for seeing that the area is left clean and in a good state of repair.*

On October 15, an exception to the time and location clause was made by giving students the Music Auditorium from 11 to 12 o'clock. Removal because of the size of the crowd to the location by the Huntington [Fighting Stallions] Statue resulted in noise, confusion, and class interruption. The Music Auditorium was offered again for November 13 but refused by the students with the statement that they did not wish administrative approval and would demonstrate on that date from 10 a.m. to 2 p.m. Many efforts over several days to effect changes in the observance of regulations were fruitless.

On Wednesday evening, November 12, the leaders were presented with a letter stating that they had not complied with regulations and that any assembly without prior approval would result in disciplinary action.

The demonstrators gathered at 10 a.m. on November 13 around the Huntington Statue. They were addressed by Dean of Students Martine and were told they had three minutes to leave or they would be suspended. All of the approximately 40 students departed the area except ten students, one faculty member, and one outsider, all of whose names were taken.

In spite of all the statements you may hear, the above is correct.

This statement was signed by Dr. Joe R. Wilson, the then–vice president for Academic Affairs. It was not well written and basically just framed the administration's version of the events. Some facts were obviously left out. For example, the original October 15 Moratorium demonstration started at the *Fighting Stallions* statue—which was not part of the designated "student expression" area—at 10:00 a.m., moved inside from 11:00 a.m. to noon and then moved back to the statue from noon to 1:00 p.m. And then there's the matter of the *Star*'s coverage of the event, which doesn't mention noise, confusion or class interruption. In fact, the *Star* portrayed the moratorium participants as composed and dignified, indicating that it was the pro-war onlookers who became raucous.

More troubling and inaccurate is the statement that indicates that the demonstration planners "did not wish administrative approval." The defining act of the October 15 Moratorium was the outdoor sit-in. In fact, the outdoor sit-in was the primary gesture of the moratorium and the crux of the group's attempt to communicate their opposition to the war. The

Admission Record
Graduate of Sealy H S 1969, Texas

Entrance Credits

Eng.	A. Hist.	W. Hist.	T. Hist.	Civi‹
G. Math.	Alg.	P. Geo.	S. Geo.	Trig
Span.	Biol.	Chem.	Gn. Sc.	Phy;
Music	Spch.	V. Ag.	M. Dr.	H.M
S. W.	Sten.	Typ.	Eco.	
Latin	Art	Jour.	Total	

ACT (St. Comp. Score)_____   Rank_____

COURSE NO.	DESCRIPTIVE TITLE	SEM HRS	LEC. HRS.	LAB. HRS.	GRADE
SUMMER II 1969					
ENG 1310	READING—WRITIN	3	7+		C
MATH 1310	BASIC MATHEMAT	3	7+		B
VYKOUKAL FRANCES A		467863270			
Enrolled Fall 1969 and Spring 1970					

COURSE NO.	DESCRIPTIVE TITLE	SEM HRS	LEC. HRS.	LAB. HRS.	GRADE
SUMMER I 1970					
ART 2310	INTR FIGURE DR	3	7+	7+	B
CHOR 1115	CHORUS	1			A
VYKOUKAL FRANCES A		467863270			

COURSE NO.	DESCRIPTIVE TITLE	SEM HRS	LEC. HRS.	LAB. HRS.	GRADE
THE SUPREME COURT OF THE UNITED STATES HAS RULED IN FAVOR OF SWTSU IN THE BAYLESS, EL AT, VS. MARTINE, EL AT, NO 71-1207 THEREFORE, CREDIT FOR THE 1969-70 SCHOOL YEAR HAS BEEN DENIED.					

Frances Vykoukal's Texas State report card. It features the wording that was placed on the San Marcos 10's transcripts after the U.S. Supreme Court refused to review a lower court ruling. *Courtesy of the University Archives, Texas State University.*

administration's "statement" suggests that Martine was trying to work with the November 13 Moratorium demonstrators, which was simply not the case. What the organizers envisioned would have been ineffective and largely irrelevant inside the Evans Auditorium. The entire point was to have the sit-in at the base of the *Fighting Stallions* statue, where it would have more public impact. The real question isn't why the protesters scoffed at administrative approval—it's why the administration suddenly forbade what it had allowed the month before.

On November 18, 1969, the San Marcos 10 appealed to the Student-Faculty Review Board, which consisted of three members of the faculty (nominated by Leland Derrick) and two students (nominated by Associated Students president Bill Miller). The faculty members were: Don Caroll Green, assistant professor of biology; Dr. James D. Elliott, professor of agriculture; and Dr. John Chatfield, assistant professor of mathematics. The students were the then-current editor of the *College Star*, Steve Blackmon, and Thomas R. Bagley. The university was represented by Martine, Derrick,

James B. Hobbs and the chief of campus security, Bill Maddox. Nine of the ten plaintiffs attended the appellate proceedings, which were held on the eleventh floor of the new Library-Administration Building. Armed campus security officers stood guard at the elevators.

The hearing began with Martine listing the incidents that led to the 10's dismissal, including the original October 15 demonstration and the meetings Martine had with the November 13 demonstration planners before the event. Then, Martine framed a question for the review: "Does the university have the right to place restrictions on the time and place of student assemblies?" The San Marcos 10's main counsel, central Texas affiliate of the ACLU, representative Mark Levbarg, noted, "Getting thrown out of school for a year's time for saying nothing and doing nothing [was] the primary point of the hearing." Brooks Holman—Michael Holman's cousin—was also a representative of the central Texas affiliate of the ACLU and was the assistant counsel for the 10. He cited two recent free speech cases in an attempt to reframe the discussion around the question: "Can the university specify forums according to the First Amendment of the Constitution of the United States?"

All nine plaintiffs in attendance testified that their constitutional rights as established in the First Amendment had been violated. When questioned why they felt they needed to protest when they did instead of during the approved periods mandated by the administration, Vykoukal stated the obvious. "There is this silent majority, and they are the ones we are trying to get to listen to us," she said. "If we would have had [the protest] at the approved time, then there wouldn't be anyone around and it would [have been] like getting in the middle of a lake and protesting where no one could see or hear you." When queried as to why they hadn't presented their grievances through the proper channels before the demonstration, Cates indicated that they had, but to no avail. "I tried to introduce a resolution into the Student Senate concerning police protection for November 13," he stated. "It was immediately killed. I was a member of that distinguished body, and I can tell you it isn't worth a damn."

Henson conceded that Martine and the administration had authority over the campus, but he suggested that the issue was bigger than that. "As citizens of the United States, we feel we had a right to sit there as long as we didn't disturb classes." Henson also pointed out that the parties responsible for any disruptions or disturbances were actually the pro-war onlookers themselves, and none of them had even received so much as "a slap on the hand." When the Review Board questioned the plaintiffs as to their "true

Vykoukal glaring at the campus security officers who were taking pictures for the administration at the November 13, 1969 Vietnam Moratorium. *Courtesy of the University Archives, Texas State University.*

intentions" for the protest, they individually and collectively indicated that they were simply exercising their First Amendment rights. "It was never our purpose to have a confrontation with the administration," Cates said, "but it has developed into that."

Ann Burleson's father was present at the appeal, and he admitted that although he didn't completely agree with his daughter's stance, he wasn't completely opposed to it either. He conceded that the students should face punitive measures, but none as drastic as a one-year suspension. He then shared something incredibly poignant for those who were really listening. "I am worried about the attitude that my daughter will come out of this with," he said. This statement from Mr. Burleson introduced a larger issue to the proceedings, one that may have been lost on the Review Board. He wasn't suggesting his daughter would have resentment toward the school itself or college in general; he was expressing concern for his daughter's very faith in American ideals. Mr. Burleson was suggesting that Annie and the rest of the 10's extreme punishment for bravely and, arguably, responsibly exercising their First Amendment rights would make them lose faith in the very principles the nation was purported to stand for.

The San Marcos 10 and their defense team made some salient points, but their appeal was denied by the Student-Faculty Review Board in a three-to-two vote. On Wednesday, November 19, the ACLU filed a civil lawsuit against Dean Martine, President Jones and the Texas State University administration (individually and collectively) in the U.S. Western District Court in Austin. In the 10's lawsuit, the ACLU maintained that the college administration had "schemed to subject" the students to a "deprivation of rights, privileges and immunities secured to them by the Constitution and the laws of the United States." The ACLU also alleged that the administration had crafted "policy which [violated] the rights of freedom of speech and assembly granted under the First and Fourteenth Amendments to the United States Constitution."

In the lawsuit, the 10 asked the university for a temporary restraining order, prohibiting their suspension prior to a final hearing in court and allowing them to return to classes, a permanent injunction preventing the university from making notations on their permanent records, a declaratory judgment that the *Hill Hints* student handbook policy dealing with student expression be void (because it was characterized by vagueness and over-breadth) and $100,000 in damages. On the morning of Thursday, November 20, Saranello and three other members of the San Marcos 10 appealed directly to President Jones. Jones denied their appeal but agreed to forward a written version of it to the Texas State University System Board of Regents. When the *Austin American-Statesman* queried Saranello afterward, he said, "We still have hopes of getting back in school."

———

Though the Student-Faculty Review Board hadn't understood or given credence to Mr. Burleson's final statement, the results of the Student Senate's referendum on the moratoriums indicated that the student body was much of the same mind as Annie and still harbored faith in American ideals. The results were released just before Thanksgiving break on the front page of the November 21 edition of the *College Star*, and the majority of the 1,500 respondents seemed to grasp what Mr. Burleson had been getting at—free

Annie Burleson taking a different approach, flashing her pearly whites for the campus security officers taking pictures at the November 13, 1969 Vietnam Moratorium. *Courtesy of the University Archives, Texas State University.*

speech is a protected right, not just a limited privilege. In regards to the question, "Do you think demonstrations have a place on campus as long as they do not infringe upon other's rights?" 75 percent of the students surveyed said "Yes." To the question, "Do you feel that recent demonstrations on SWTSU campus are infringing upon your rights?" 71 percent said "No." The resultant *Star* editorial, "'Silent Majority' Lashes Out," was entirely unsympathetic to the pro-war student senators who had incorrectly assumed that the student body shared their contempt for the protesters:

> *The Silent Majority at SWT has spoken. And what they had to say was not at all what their loudest boosters had expected.*
>
> *The Silent Majority stood up for student rights by an overwhelming majority in Wednesday's referendum, and, in doing so, repudiated those people who have been using their name to oppose student demonstrations.*
>
> *The original backers of the referendum made no secret of the fact that they expected the Silent Majority to come through in their denunciation of the Vietnam Moratorium. But the idea backfired on them....One Student Senator who backed the referendum said the vote would show the* College

In a 1985 interview, Texas State history professor Richard B. Henderson said that the San Marcos 10 had a good case, but the university won by resorting to "subterfuge." *From the 1969 Pedagog yearbook.*

Star *how the student body feels about Vietnam Moratoriums and such demonstrations. We now know. Thank you.*

The November 21 edition of the *Star* also reported that Student Senator Ed Huth had introduced a resolution that stated the Student Senate "[deplored] the action taken by the administration of the school regarding the peaceful moratorium activities on Vietnam, which took place on the morning of Thursday, November 13, 1969." The resolution was tabled after senior Student Senator Sheldon Padgett—who had taken part in the arguably more disruptive San Marcos Veteran's Day Parade[68] two days before the November 13 Moratorium—objected to its consideration and threatened to filibuster it.

The most powerful part of the November 21 *Star*, however, was a "Reader's Pulse" letter to the editor from David Basye of the University News Service. Titled "Attacks Not Right," it cryptically addressed the *Star* editor, Steve Blackmon, himself:

> *You will be next. Since concerned students risked suspension last year protesting against Mr. McCrocklin's plagiarism, the administration has*

continually attempted to dominate attitudes, issues and events, and pervert them to fit their own goals....They don't like attacks, true or otherwise....

Dr. Jones is a good and sincere man. However, he has been led astray by those who backed McCrocklin. They are childish. They must have their way.

I have been a professional news man for this university for nearly two years. I have always fought for the administration since they pay me for my services. I have been closer, know more and am more ashamed for this campus than most people. I know I will lose my job for this. But that is the way the administration does things.

A lot of people have suffered for what they believe. God bless them for trying. We will all lose. And, this is not about the war issue, it is the freedom of speech issue. Why should we be any different from the Negro, the Mexican-American or the poor? All we have is a belief—they have the means to suppress those beliefs. God save them. But, you, Mr. Editor, will be next. You will be fired....

On Monday, November 24, 1969, the San Marcos 10's appeal to the Texas State University System Board of Regents was denied. Dean Martine was present, and during the proceedings, he conceded that the San Marcos 10 were not disruptive themselves during the November 13 demonstration. However, he also noted that the protest organizers had requested a campus security presence, so they must have "expected a disruption."

"We've never had anything like this," Martine testified. "If we are not in a situation where we can tell them not to have it in an area where it is disruptive, we're in a sad state of affairs."

10

DEAN-SPLAINING

I found the university clean and noble, but I did not find the university alive.
—Jack London, American novelist, journalist and social activist

In several incidents and discussions of rape in the last few decades, girls and women have often been blamed for what happened to them because they wore something sexy, revealing, i.e., inviting. This argument is pathetic, asinine and odious, because it is predicated on the notion that boys and men in general can't be expected to control themselves. A lack of self-control and a rush to unaccountability are secondary considerations to the actual victim's caution in terms of fashion. It is the essence of a ridiculous and still widely held patriarchal mandate that, somehow, straight-facedly proclaims that since men and boys can't control themselves, girls and women should not wear skimpy, tight apparel. *And if they do, they're asking for it. And if they're asking for it, they just may get it. And if something happens to them—isn't it, in some way, their fault?*

No member of the San Marcos 10 was raped by Texas State or members of its administration, but it's hard not to consider that the same rationale was used in their case when examining one of Dean Floyd Martine's comments at the Friday, November 28, 1969 U.S. Western District Court hearing. When finally addressing why the Texas State administration had refused to give the November 13 Moratorium planners permission to demonstrate at the *Fighting Stallions* statue after they had deemed it acceptable the month before, Martine claimed the protest in October disrupted classes in the surrounding buildings. However, since he had already conceded in previous hearings that the demonstrators themselves were not disruptive, he went on to clarify the issue: "The SWT Rodeo Cowboys' Association had expressed a great deal of animosity, and we were afraid if there was another demonstration at the same time and the same place, there would be a great deal of trouble."

The Texas State administration was clearly "man-splaining" or, in Martine's case, "dean-splaining" to the court. Their implied assumption was—as in the case of rapists—that the SWT Rodeo Club and related pro-war elements on campus harbored impulses that they couldn't control, and it would be unwise and perhaps even dangerous to tempt them. President Billy Mac Jones played along, testifying, "As an administrator, it makes little difference to me how violence starts—it's my job to prevent it." Dr. William C. Pool, a speaker at the indoor portion of the October 15 demonstration, testified at the hearing. He stated that he had experienced fear for his own safety at the event—but in regards to the pro-war antagonists, not the antiwar demonstrators.[69]

ACLU attorneys Levbarg and Holman challenged the administration's stance, pointing out that the campus rules regarding these matters "were not enforced equally," noting that five hundred students had gathered on the edge of campus to take part in the Veteran's Day festivities two days before the November 13 Moratorium protest. They also cited the court cases: *Tinker v. Des Moines Community School District* (1969), which found that "peaceful, orderly, campus assemblies for the purpose of political demonstration are protected 1st Amendment activities"; and *Schneider v. New Jersey* (1939), which found that "one is not to have the exercise of his liberty of expression in appropriate places abridged on the plea that it may be exercised in some other place."

Along with the appeal from the San Marcos 10, the ACLU filed five affidavits: four from fellow students (eighteen-year-old Paula Gene Clift, twenty-three-year-old Luise Maddox, twenty-five-year-old Fred S. Schwartz and thirty-one-year-old Nancy Hanks Ellis, whose husband was the Hays County Republican chair), which indicated that the San Marcos 10 had been "peaceful and orderly" and "did not disrupt any classes or campus activities." The fifth affidavit came from a Travis County notary public named Lois P. Sulsar. Sulsar affirmed that Martine had acknowledged at the November 18 Student-Faculty Review Board that the 10 had demonstrated "in a peaceful and orderly fashion" and had not interfered "with classes or campus traffic." She also pointed out that the plaintiffs and their counsel had not been "permitted to cross-examine witnesses against them" at the Review Board hearing.

U.S. District Court judge Jack Roberts heard arguments from both sides; he decided to rule on the matter and consider a temporary injunction (that might allow the San Marcos 10 to return to school) at a later date.

———

On Monday, December 1, Texas State students returned from Thanksgiving break, and previous "Reader's Pulse" letters proved prescient. Steve Blackmon was removed as editor of the *College Star*, and a number of the staff resigned in protest. The Student Court subsequently declared that the Student Senate's October 13, 1969 statement that "anyone wanting to participate in local action involving U.S. involvement [in Vietnam] on Oct. 15, 1969, should be permitted to do so without penalty or prejudice" was unconstitutional.

At the Associated Student Government meeting that Monday evening, Student Senator Kent Garrett resigned "due to the suspension of 10 SWTSU students and the events surrounding this outrage, and due to the Student Senate's failure to respond to this action."

After an executive report by the Associated Student Government president, Bill Miller, Garrett shared a statement:

> *I feel it is my responsibility as a member of this body to illuminate the fact that no positive action has been taken to insure those students' [the San Marcos 10] reinstatement in SWTSU.*
>
> *Therefore, feeling that the students of this college, whom this august body is supposed to represent, have no voice in the future of the institution, I resign from the office of off-campus senator immediately.*
>
> *I would like to add that I feel the majority of the fault for this does not lie in the organization of the Senate or any of its members but rather from the power structure of the university system.*

Then, Garrett shrugged his shoulders and quietly exited the senate chamber.

These days, Garrett still shrugs his shoulders. In a December 2018 interview, he indicated that he still recalled this period with frustration:

I ran for office in order to represent a growing contingent of students who were fed up with the status quo. The U.S. presence in Southeast Asia was increasingly unpopular on campus and seemed in need of redress. So, when the Student Senate refused to address the issues at hand by ignoring bill after bill on the subject, it became clear that further attempts to change this forum seemed an exercise in futility. The Student Senate was more concerned with innocuous local issues of superficial concern and ignored any attempts to be relevant to the affairs of the day.

Award-winning *University Star* editor Steve Blackmon (*right*) was forced to resign after conservative elements around campus complained about the newspaper's "biased" reporting. *From the 1969* Pedagog *yearbook.*

When the first post-editorial purge edition of the *Star* appeared on December 5, 1969, the paper was clearly a bit more bland, but some of the students involved still let slip some "Reader's Pulse" submissions that probably kept the censors on edge. Recent graduate Wendell Jackson lamented a "tragedy" at Texas State:

As an August 1969 graduate of SWTSU, I cannot help being concerned about the recent suspension of ten students there for exercising what I consider to be their human right to peaceful dissent. I condemn the Viet Nam [sic] slaughter and vigorously support the right of these students to express their aversion to this war.

The university rule which requires forty-eight hours prior approval by the dean allows Dean Martine to suppress any demonstration that he does not personally agree with. That old catch-all provision about the demonstration "disrupting classes" is as ambiguous, flagrant and untenable as the "disorderly conduct" statutes which permit policemen and magistrates to abridge the Negro's right to demonstrate against the state status quo that has oppressed him for so many decades.

It is time for those students, faculty members and administrators who defend a college president's right to plagiarize to ask themselves why they grant one person the right to dishonesty while abridging another person's right to freedom of expression. What a tragedy for SWTSU.

Then, Texas State instructor Ronald M. Sawey took the administration to task for its selective tolerance for disruptions:

If I understand the Administration's position correctly, one of the principal reasons for denying the requested time and place for the moratorium demonstration on November 13 was that, on October 15, the result was "noise, confusion and class interruptions."

On this subject of "noise, confusion, and class interruptions," it might be worthwhile to consider the following examples of classes being disturbed—disturbed sometimes to the point of forcing an early dismissal of class: (1) Hammering and banging from workmen in adjacent rooms; (2) Faulty or nonexistent air conditioning necessitating the opening of windows with the ensuing din from the air compressors at the Flowers Hall renovation and Strahan Gym sandblasting; (3) Repairmen entering a class in session and going to work with their pipe wrenches; (4) Clanging "steam hammers" from antiquated heating systems.

*If we can patiently endure these and other inconveniences in the name of
"progress" or "necessity," then why can we not tolerate disturbances such as
moratorium demonstrations replete with hecklers, et al.—disturbances that
are no more noisy and certainly less frequent than the others—in the name
of "freedom of expression?"*[70]

In a letter titled "Forum Requested," students Mary Hazard and
Chuck Jones called out the final line of Dean Joe R. Wilson's November
14 administration statement, opining that the claim, "In spite of all other
statements you may hear, the above are correct," was actually incorrect and
misleading, and the suggestion that the "main objective" of the moratorium
demonstrators was "direct confrontation with the administration" was
patently false. Hazard and Jones then requested that a forum—not unlike the
previous one regarding McCrocklin—be held between the demonstrators
and faculty so that members of the majority of the campus community
could "see for themselves what the true situation is." There is no evidence
that the administration ever entertained the idea of a student-faculty forum
to get to the bottom of how the moratorium and San Marcos 10 issues were
being handled at Texas State.

In early December, after the editorial purge, a prescribed incuriousness
found purchase in the weekly coverage and opinion pieces of the *College
Star*. Under acting editor Jane Howard, the main editorials became
conspicuously administration-friendly and supportive of the war effort. A
prominent opinion piece in the December 12, 1969 edition of the *Star*,
titled "Dissenter's Efforts in Vain?" suggested that the antiwar movement
had done nothing except give comfort to our enemies and "prolong the
Vietnam slaughter."

But if the pro-war elements of the administration, faculty, staff and student
body began breathing sighs of relief, their respite was brief. Former *Star*
managing editor Bill Cunningham started a new, underground newspaper
called the *Purgatory Creek Press (PCP)* and brought along *Star* editorial
cartoonist Kent Garrett. The *PCP*'s gloves-off, underground approach to
events at Texas State was refreshing, and its December 9, 1969 coverage of
Garrett's Student Senate resignation was a little more colorful than the *Star*'s
had been:

*During last Monday night's Senate meeting, Senator Kent Garrett, erstwhile
P.C.P. staffer and chromosome-damaged maddog campus revolutionary,
announced his resignation from the position of off-campus senator. Garrett*

President Johnson visited his alma mater several times after he left office. This trip was in April 1970. That's Texas State president Billy Mac Jones to his left and Leland Derrick just over Johnson's left shoulder. *From the 1969* Pedagog *yearbook.*

> *left his post because of the total ineffectiveness of the so-called "Student" Senate in standing up for the students of Southwest Texas. In his resignation, he charged the responsibility for the Senate's ineptness lies with its power structure, which sees a few administration apologists exerting control over a group of mindless puppets*
>
> *Meanwhile, the Senate remained mired in its usual bog of mediocrity.*
>
> *The funniest moment of the year came three weeks ago when [Student] Senator Pat Corbin reminded his constituents that they [the senators] represent the student body and should therefore not pass a bill condemning the administration for its totalitarian actions November 13. Pat is famous for representing the student body about as much as George Wallace[71] represents Harlem. Right on, Pat.*

PCP's December 9, 1969 coverage of the Student-Faculty Review Board's decision regarding the San Marcos 10 was even more riotous. Here is an excerpt:

This board was neatly stacked with professors from the Math, Science, and Agriculture departments. (A coincidence that none of 'em were from the liberal arts?) One of the two students was a John Birch–type.

The chairman of this Kangaroo Court was Dr. Elliott, who must have spent a good deal of time studying Judge Julius Hoffman[72] of Chicago. Elliott's questions to the students made it obvious that his mind was made up before he entered the room, and, of course, the board ruled against the students.

Ole [Leland] Derrick, vice-president of the university and acting president was there slobbering about and finally making a dumbass statement about how the ten students were at fault for any disturbance that observers caused.

In early December, U.S. District Court judge Jack Roberts denied the 10's appeal for reinstatement but did not rule on the merits of the case, noting that "no party denies that the First Amendment applies with full vigor on the campus, but a university, by reasonable regulation, can limit and regulate the exercise of rights granted by the Constitution." The 10 immediately appealed Roberts's denial to the Fifth U.S. Circuit Court of Appeals in New Orleans, and on Friday, December 12, the Fifth Circuit temporarily blocked the students' suspension "pending the disposition of this appeal and subject to further orders." On Monday, December 15, eight of the San Marcos 10 returned to their studies at Texas State. McConchie had moved to New Mexico with his wife and daughter, and Al Henson had joined a rock band and gone on tour.

On Tuesday, December 16, two dozen Texas State students staged a third Vietnam Moratorium at the *Fighting Stallions* statue. The *PCP*'s January 6, 1970 coverage was in and of the moment:

The December 16 Moratorium demonstration last month came off with no casualties, but it took some nomadic demonstrators to foil the plans of Dean of Students Floyd Martine (known affectionately as Smilin' Floyd).

The night before the moratorium, slated [to take place] in front of the Huntington [Fighting Stallions] statues, Martine delivered a letter to moratorium representative Kent Garrett, informing him that participants in the December Moratorium would face the same consequences as those in November, when ten students were suspended from SWT by Smilin' Floyd only to be returned a month later by order of a federal judge.

So, at 11 a.m. [on] December 16, there are about 50 demonstrators standing around the statue, waiting anxiously for Martine to appear.

Suddenly, Ralph Longoria, the Paul Revere of the Damaged Chromosome set, comes running down the Quad shouting, "The fascists are coming! The fascists are coming!"

And sure enough, here came Martine, all six feet and 38 teeth of him, with his little entourage of dour-faced lower echelon administrators and Kodak clicking campus cops.

But just as the dean reached the demonstrators, all but two of them stood, turned their backs to him and walked away.

Martine then read his letter to the remaining duo, informing them they had five minutes to clear the area or be suspended.

When asked why he had extended the time limit from the three minute ultimatum given the previous month, the witty administrator replied, "I'm getting liberal in my old age."

The two-person, class-disrupting mob then moved, but, by then, another problem faced Martine.

All the demonstrators who had walked off resettled in the grassy area between the sidewalks of Evans Academic Center and the Fine Arts Building, only a few yards from where they were originally.

Texas State antiwar protesters sitting at the base of the *Fighting Stallions* statue at one of the Vietnam moratoriums. *Courtesy of the University Archives, Texas State University.*

But according to Martine's own rules, an unauthorized demonstration is one that has been planned beforehand and which he has vetoed. Therefore, by the dean's own admission, the people sitting on the grass were not holding a "demonstration" but a "gathering."

Frustrated by the fact that the demonstrators were becoming as adept as the administration at using red tape, Martine then returned to his office.

So, for the rest of the morning, the "gathering" participants sat around posing for pictures and smiling like their hero.

But you could tell that without the friendly dean around, some of the fun had gone out of the whole thing.

According to the *Dallas Morning News*, one of the December 16 protesters asked Martine what he was going to do about the protesters resuming their demonstration after the abrupt relocation. "I came here because I read in the paper that some students were going to hold an unauthorized demonstration at the *Stallion*," Martine replied. "They have disbanded. I can't go around and ask everyone what they are doing."

The demonstration lasted from just after 11:00 a.m. to 1:00 p.m.

ILLUSIONS

The American soldiers were brave, but courage is not enough. David did not kill Goliath just because he was brave. He looked up at Goliath and realized that if he fought Goliath's way, with a sword, Goliath would kill him. But, if he picked up a rock and put it in his sling, he could hit Goliath in the head and knock Goliath down and kill him. David used his mind when he fought Goliath. So did we Vietnamese when we had to fight the Americans.[73]
—*Vo Nguyen Giap, Vietnamese general and politician*

If you grab a copy of Texas State University's now daily *University Star*, the slogan on the masthead reads, "Defending the First Amendment Since 1911." It sounds good, but it's not true.

As discussed in chapter five, *Star* editor Porter Sparkman was expressly forbidden to publish editorials on Lyndon B. Johnson's policies and was warned off of stories that were critical of McCrocklin and the university. This was just a primer for the brazen measures that would be taken to silence *Star* staffers following the first two Vietnam moratorium demonstrations in late 1969. After the *Star*'s coverage of the November 13 protest and the suspension of the San Marcos 10, any pretense of freedom of the press at Texas State was utterly obliterated. As noted in the last chapter, however, the victims of the administration's *Star* purge were not without a voice.

In the January 6, 1969 edition of the *PCP*, students at Texas State got a firsthand account of the matter from former *Star* managing editor Bill Cunningham, who was then at the helm of the *PCP*. The cover of that issue of the *PCP* featured a headstone. The headstone inscription read, "R.I.P. The *College Star.*" The Cunningham article that explained the front cover was titled "The Death of a Student Newspaper":

> *While covering the October 15 Moratorium at Southwest Texas, I was approached by one of the demonstrators who asked me what paper I was working for. When I told him, "The College Star," he replied, "You guys have a lot of guts to be trying to put out a liberal paper on this campus." I merely shrugged that statement off. Why should it take "guts" to establish a liberal editorial policy on a college newspaper? Freedom of the press applies to the college press too, doesn't it?*
>
> *Three months later, I can't say whether it was guts, obstinance or strong whiskey that carried the Star's editorial staff through the semester, but I can say this: freedom of press is a myth at Southwest Texas (Texas State).*
>
> *The war of intimidation that was waged on the Star editors by Journalism Department Chairman Dr. Frank Buckley and his cohorts was enough to distroy [sic] anyone's illusions about freedom of the press. Harassing criticism, veiled innuendo and just plain lying were the weapons used to finally cut down the Star editorship.*
>
> *Before proceeding any further, perhaps we should look back to the Star of years past. The most controversial subject discussed on the campus in the editorial page was who should pick up the litter off the campus.*[74] *The Star was always solidly behind apple pie, the American flag, and motherhood…*
>
> *So, when the Star came out in support of the October 15 Moratorium, it surprised quite a few people, including me—and I wrote the editorial.*
>
> *It was at this time that Dr. Buckley began to express his concerns about the political beliefs of the Star staff. Could they be under the influence of the "liberal element" on campus?*
>
> *At that time, Star editor Steve Blackmon vowed to quit if Buckley began to interfere with The College Star's right to express opinions. Several others of us said we would join him. We felt that a united staff would insure our rights, and we were confident that we were all united. Nobody then knew how much Jane Howard wanted to be editor to The College Star.*
>
> *Later editorials did little to alleviate Buckley's anxieties, and, on November 3, the investigation was sprung on us.*
>
> *Ironically, the first step taken to eliminate students' freedom of the press was taken by a body of students supposedly representing students.*

After the Texas State administration purged the *University Star* of "biased" editors in late 1969, underground publications sprung up around campus. The first was the *Purgatory Creek Press*. The second was the *Weather Report*. *From the 1971* Pedagog *yearbook.*

On that day, in the Student Senate, David Bowman introduced a resolution, charging the Star *with contributing to campus unrest and demanding an investigation by the Publications Committee. The resolution passed.*

The Publications Committee met a week later. The committee is headed by Dr. Buckley, who notifies the committee members when meetings are to be held. One of the two student members of the committee is Pam Smisek, who was also one of the "liberal" Star *editors at the time. She was not notified of the meeting. I managed to contact her only minutes before the closed session was scheduled to begin.*

What happened that afternoon was no investigation. A better word would be "kangaroo court." Its purpose was to fire Steve Blackmon as editor of the Star. *But the* Star *had its defenders at the meeting, too, and they managed to block the takeover attempt. It was only a stay of execution.*

Buckley began spending more and more time in closed door meetings; many with Jane Howard, the editor of the yearbook and editorial assistant on the Star.

Rumors began anew that the editor would be fired, and, on Monday, December 9, Buckley got the break he had been waiting for. On that day, a girl who is well-known in the Journalism Department met with Buckley and told him that Blackmon and other editors were using drugs.

It was a known fact that this girl [had] hated Blackmon for over a year, but her word was taken. Truth was not the point. The mere suspicion of drugs would have been enough for the Board of Regents to dismiss Blackmon. So, rather than face the stigma of a firing, Blackmon resigned.

Two other staff members, news editor Pam Smisek and cartoonist Kent Garrett, also submitted resignations in outrage at the depths to which the battle had descended.

Jane Howard was named acting editor of the Star *by Buckley, to no one's surprise, despite the fact that under the proper line of succession, the managing editor is supposed to fill the position.*

Even though I knew my days were numbered, I decided not to quit. I felt by making them fire me, they would have to hand me a reason. And I've got to hand it to Buckley and Jane Howard—the way they got rid of me was outrageously masterful.

The Star *prints on Thursdays at the* San Marcos Record. *This particular Thursday, I arrived, as usual, Thursday afternoon. I stayed there all afternoon, even after I discovered my name had been removed from the masthead. I had still received no notification of dismissal when I left for dinner that night.*

While I was gone, I later learned from a Record *employee, Buckley had called and talked to the* Record *publisher, Addison Buckner. Upon my return, the elderly Buckner confronted me at the door.*

"Are you working for the Star," *he gruffly asked.*

In view of the removal of my name from the masthead, I jokingly replied, "I'm not sure."

His jowls quivering, Buckner called out, "Well then get out." He wasn't joking.

Knowing that the police would be called if I stayed, I left. Two more staffers, news editor Linda Haster and sports columnist Bill Walker, decided that they had had enough of this viciousness and walked out, too.

And so, now, if you ask Dr. Buckley why I was fired from managing editor of the Star, *he can say it was because of "dereliction of duties." I was derelict in my duties by not being at the* Record *Thursday night.*

The really ludicrous thing that happened was after I left, when the doors of the Record *were locked. Buckley showed up, as did the campus police.*

According to a witness who was there, they (the people at the Record*) were afraid we might attack with a bomb or lead a guerilla attack.*

The funny part stops though when Buckley tries to get me through my family.

In a telephone conversation with my father, Buckley told him I was coming to class so stoned from drugs that my eyes were all bloodshot and red. Having known me for quite a while, however, my father was aware that I suffered from hay-fever, which severely irritates my eyes for much of the winter. You would think a man with a law degree, as Buckley has, would know better than to make charges like that without a medical report. But, as I said earlier, truth is not the point.

In that same conversation, Buckley charged that I might even be so radical as to be associated with the Black Panthers. It was the first I heard of the Black Panthers being in San Marcos. Anyway, my parents agree with me that my politics are none of Buckley's business…

The Star *has now returned to its status as a top-notch high school paper. The liberals have been removed, and Steve Blackmon and Pam Smisek are leaving school.*

Purged editor Steve Blackmon's helm of the *College Star* that autumn earned it recognition as an All-American Paper.

Not long after the *PCP* started publishing, its staffers began experiencing harassment. On one occasion, Dean Martine showed up at the front door of Garrett's off-campus residence with a campus security escort to send a warning to Garrett and his coworkers about publishing the *PCP*. San Marcos 10 participants David Bayless and Murray Rosenwasser were both contributors to *PCP* at one time or another, and it would be published for close to a year before being replaced by John Pfeffer's *Weather Report*. In late 1970, student journalists writing for what would then be called the *University Star* were prohibited from moonlighting at the *Weather Report*. At one point, however, even tenured Texas State professors were submitting editorials concerning the administration's treatment of the San Marcos 10 to the *Report*.[75]

———

Under the conditions of the injunction, the San Marcos 10 finished the fall semester of 1969 and the spring semester of 1970.

In mid-February, Saranello, acting on behalf of a significant portion of the student body, met with university officials and requested that an open discussion be held between the administration and the students regarding the policies around faculty tenure, promotions, hirings and terminations. His concerns were ignored. Later that same year, Saranello reached out to progressive state senator A.R. "Babe" Schwartz[76] and invited him to speak at Texas State after a moratorium they were planning for April.

On Wednesday, April 15, 1970, Schwartz made an appearance at Texas State, but he didn't exactly observe the normal formalities. First, 150 students holding umbrellas, wrapped in blankets and carrying antiwar signs gathered in the Quad for another Vietnam moratorium demonstration. They then joined another 50 students, faculty members and administrators in the Fine Arts Auditorium to hear Schwartz speak. "It didn't get unpopular to be a radical until the Vietnam War," Schwartz said. "It never became treason until that time. From World War II to the Vietnam War, to speak out against the government of the United States was one of our great privileges. The Vietnam War caused this great cleavage in our society." Schwartz also pointed out that protesting wasn't enough, that young people and antiwar demonstrators needed to organize and oppose pro-war politicians at every level, from their student government to the national government in Washington, D.C.

After the rally, Schwartz briefly met with Texas State dignitaries (like President Jones) but reserved his dinner plans for the San Marcos 10. The members who were still present in the area gathered at a house that Bayless and Rosenwasser were renting and had spaghetti and meatballs with the senator.

LBJ also made a visit to the Texas State campus in April. The former POTUS's hair was longer, and he looked tired, but he seemed to enjoy the visit. Paul Cates recalled proudly shaking his hand. Satagaj, Rosenwasser and others remembered something else.

At one moment during a short tour of the campus, President Jones made a special point to apologize to Johnson for the recent protests. Johnson's response was as surprising as it was succinct.

"They were right," Johnson said, without explanation or elaboration.

Jones pursued the matter no further.

By late spring 1970, President Nixon and his staff had moved past their self-serving, half-baked psychological diagnosis of the nation's protesting youth and openly viewed them as hostiles. On Monday, May 4, 1970—three days after President Richard Nixon referred to antiwar protesters at the nation's colleges and universities as "bums"—the Ohio National Guard engaged a Kent State University demonstration in Kent, Ohio, and shot nine students, killing four and paralyzing one for life. Former Texas State professor William I. Gorden was there. "I was on campus, but I didn't see the shooting," Gorden said. "The National Guard troops had the students surrounded. The school was eventually shut down. For a while, I taught classes in my barn."

The State of Ohio initially pressed charges against the protesting Kent State students—not the Guardsmen. Gorden went on to support the Kent 25 (the twenty-four students and one faculty member charged) and taped over 150 interviews with witnesses of the shooting. His tapes were later used in a number of successful wrongful death lawsuits against the governor of Ohio, the president of Kent State University and the National Guardsmen involved.

At 9:30 a.m. on the morning of Wednesday, May 6, Saranello and Texas State sophomore Mike Owens led a march through the Quad, protesting the student deaths at Kent State. Some pro-war students attempted to block the march's path along a few of the sidewalks, but attentive bystanders called the would-be obstructers out and told them to move and let the forty-five-person procession pass. The group of protesters grew to include students carrying signs and sitting in the grassy areas while chanting, "Peace now! Peace now!"

At approximately 10:10 a.m., Bill Maddox, the head of campus security, and James B. Hobbs, assistant to the president, arrived to break the protest up, but Dean Floyd Martine suddenly appeared and countermanded their decision. "Let them walk around," Martine said.

Soon, a growing contingent of Texas State students began to feel that the American flag should be lowered to half-staff to recognize the Kent State tragedy. On Thursday, May 7, Bayless, Saranello, Satagaj and Rosenwasser, along with several other students, approached the flag area on the Quad to survey the prospects of such a venture. A gathering of cowboys was waiting, and they began to bluster and hurl insults at the group. Then, an unidentified student that neither Bayless, Saranello, Satagaj nor Rosenwasser recognized began urging them to tear the Stars and Stripes down.[77] The engagement quickly verged on becoming a serious physical altercation, and the San Marcos 10 participants braced for the worst. Then, something curious occurred. Saranello began singing "America the Beautiful." The other members of the 10 and the cowboys joined in.

Once the song ended, the two groups started talking. When the cowboys learned that Rosenwasser had been in the military and that Bayless had actually served in Vietnam, tempers cooled. "You could feel the intensity go down," Bayless recalled. "A calm spread through both sides, and it became an educational moment. The two groups broke down into smaller groups and talked. And really listened. We became quiet and respectful, and it was a great feeling."

———◆———

In an editorial titled "Murder at Kent U.; Panty Raid at SWT" in the May 8, 1970 edition of the *Star*, editorial assistant James McConnell touched on the murdered students at Kent State, then juxtaposed it with the scene at Texas State:

> *Meanwhile, at SWT, male students are fighting desperately for the pairs of flimsy undergarments that come floating down from the windows of Falls and Sterry Hall. Cheers can be heard from as far off as Summitt House as the roving bands of passion-inflamed men go plundering off in search of a fresh supply of dainty delights.*
>
> *Earthshattering news, isn't it? While students are being shot demonstrating against a war that they are morally against and buildings are being burned in protest, the world seems to be standing still here at San Marcos; instead of becoming involved in the direction and possible future of the world, we are being represented as a school that's biggest excitement and movement of participation is a panty raid!*

On the evening of May 9, a small group of Texas State students (including Michael Holman) marched on President Jones's residence in an attempt to speak with him about Kent State. The president politely declined. On the evening of May 11, a larger group of Texas State students—organized by Saranello and Owens again—returned to Jones's residence and presented him with an unsigned, handwritten statement:

> *1. We students at SWT request of President Jones to hold Wednesday, May 13, as a day of mourning for all people who have died by violence, especially our brothers and sisters killed at Kent State and in Southeast*

Asia. We ask for a simple lowering of the flag to half-mast as an act of respect for those who have died. We further ask that President Jones declare this day a day of reflection and a day to be used by faculty members and students for discussion on the tragic events of the past few weeks.

2. We ask that President Jones, on behalf of the students at SWT, express our deepest concern to President Nixon over the recent somber events and that we are against the President's moving into Cambodia and the National Guard's actions at Kent State [University], Ohio. We feel the need for these simple requests to show that our university is concerned and aware over issues that touch our very lives, to show in some mild form that this institution holds a place for thought and humanity. Also, that the concerns of all students are considered and acted upon fairly by this administration.

Saranello received President Jones's response at approximately 1:30 p.m. on Tuesday, May 12:

Last evening, for the second time in three nights, I was visited by a group of students asking we establish an institutional posture regarding this nation's foreign policies and domestic crises.

This academic community serves a variety of constituencies shading off to a variety of beliefs and opinions, with each constituency thinking that its beliefs and opinions are those most appropriate for the occasion and, thus, should be made official institutional policy.

This we will not do.

Students at Southwest Texas State enjoy an open and liberal cut policy regarding class absences. It is handled on the basis of individual option; therefore, any student whose conscience dictates that he observe tomorrow as a day of mourning is free to exercise [that] option and absent himself from class. To decree a day of no classes would be to thrust an equally unwanted action on an equally sincere group and thereby invade their rights and freedoms.

With regard to the request of lowering the flag: the position of the flag is determined by federal precedent, not local pleasure. The nation's flag responds to a national will and we at Southwest Texas fly our flag in accordance with whatever instructions are sent to federal installations around the world.

Our students and our staff are concerned over those events which shape our destinies and effect our lives so closely and so deeply, but the name of the University is not the proper vehicle for giving expression to these concerns.

Three days later, on May 15, 1970, city and state police shot fourteen antiwar demonstrators at Jackson State University in Jackson, Mississippi, killing two.

In the summer of 1970, the Fifth U.S. Circuit Court of Appeals ruled in favor of Texas State, stating that the school had acted within its rights when it suspended the San Marcos 10. The 10 appealed the Fifth U.S. Circuit Court of Appeals decision to the U.S. Supreme Court, and they filed a second suit to force Texas State University to grant them credit for the classwork they completed over the 1969–70 school year.

Early in the fall of 1970, another group of college students in Texas ran into an even more Draconian restriction of speech (or student expression) at Tyler Junior College (in Tyler, Texas) when they attempted to register for classes. Approximately forty young men were refused admittance to the school because their hair lengths were considered "disruptive" and did not conform to the college dress code. Most of these "long-hair" students left and got haircuts before reapplying or just applied elsewhere. Several didn't enroll anywhere at all. However, three of these students— Joe R. Lansdale, Paul Harden and L.H. Hutchinson—hired a lawyer and filed suit, claiming that "the enforcement by college officials of such regulation against them was arbitrary and unreasonable and violated their constitutional rights."

In October 1970, the United States Eastern District Court in Tyler, Texas, granted an injunction against Tyler Junior College, allowing the plaintiffs to enroll. The Memorandum Opinion stated that no evidence presented at the hearing justified "the belief that an individual with long hair will change dramatically in character once his hair is shortened" and that a regulation "designed to eliminate all male students with long hair as a deterrent to disruption, is unreasonable, discriminatory, and void."

"It wasn't a protest until they made it one," says Lansdale, now an accomplished, well-known Texas author.[78] "The policy was representative of the past, and it was time for a change."

———◆———

In early November 1970, flyers began appearing around the Texas State campus announcing a silent protest on the same Thursday the San Marcos 10 had protested the year before:

People,

I am not proud that only twenty-five Americans lost their life in Vietnam last week. What saddens me is that almost one thousand human beings were killed last week in an unjust war. So, on November 12, between twelve and one o'clock, I will sit in silent protest as the rest of the San Marcos 10 and I did one year ago. Nixon cannot sacrifice human beings for the political phrase "Honorable Peace." I am still resolved that we should end the war, and end it now. No school administration can silence my silence.
Join me,
Michael Holman

Holman told the *University Star* that even though the number of U.S. soldiers involved in Vietnam had decreased, the killing was still going on. "As far as I'm concerned," Holman said, "you can't justify Napalm bombing no matter what you do....I can't see that anything has changed." Before the silent, one-year anniversary sit-in occurred, pro-war elements on campus began taking down

Michael Holman led an antiwar demonstration the day before the one-year anniversary of the San Marcos 10 protest. *From the 1971* Pedagog *yearbook.*

the flyers and destroying them. When the protest did occur, however, there were no heckling cowboys and no one was threatened or suspended. Two campus security officers observed from a short distance, but there was no disturbance.

In January 1971, the San Marcos 10's school credit suit landed once again in the chamber of the U.S. Federal Western District Court, and Judge Jack Roberts again ruled against the 10, stating that he could see no constitutional justification for countermanding the conclusion of the Fifth U.S. Circuit Court of Appeals. "I have nothing but sympathy for anyone who has worked in classes and loses credit," Roberts said. "Frankly, I wish there was some way I could help these people have their grades, but we know what the law is, according to the circuit court. I'd have to set the law aside and say we'll just ignore it this time."

In May 1972, the San Marcos 10 suspension appeal was submitted to the U.S. Supreme Court, but only Justice William Douglas voted to review the case. The highest court in the land let the lower court's ruling stand, and the San Marcos 10 lost all of the credits they earned during the 1969–70 school year. Their official transcripts still read, "The U.S. Supreme Court has ruled for the administration, and all credit is denied." Saranello was not surprised. "The university administrators felt the protests were very embarrassing," he said. "They wanted to make sure it never happened again. They still felt they could rule with an iron hand, and they did not like being second-guessed. They wanted to punish the participants, so they did."

On October 4, 1972, in the matter of *Tyler Junior College v. Lansdale*, Lansdale, Harden and Hutchinson fared much better than the San Marcos 10. The Fifth Circuit Court of Appeals ruled that it was "constitutionally impermissible for a state junior college to adopt and enforce a regulation prescribing the length or grooming or style of a male student's hair." The court's decision also stated that a college campus "marks the boundary of the area within which a student's hirsute adornment becomes constitutionally irrelevant to the pursuit of educational activities." In other words, primary and secondary schools were permitted to police or mandate hairstyles—but colleges and universities were not.

On March 29, 1973, American combat troops were withdrawn from Vietnam.

On May 14, 1973, the U.S. Supreme Court refused to hear Tyler Junior College's appeal and let the Fifth Circuit Court's ruling on "long-hairs" at the college level stand. "We were determined," Lansdale said. "And I'm proud of the fact that I was involved." Lansdale himself refused to go to Vietnam;

but the military decided it would be simpler to give him a psychological deferment than prosecute. One of Lansdale's most beloved characters, Hap Collins—from his *Hap and Leonard* book and TV series—is a man after his creator's mind. Hap is a working-class Texan who, in his youth, chose federal prison time over serving in Vietnam.

AWFUL BROOD OF PREJUDICE

When we say Truth is the inveterate enemy of error and its train of evil, we say that it is the foe of ignorance also. It is in the darkness of ignorance that intolerance grows, with its awful brood of prejudice, persecution and strife.
—*Lyndon Baines Johnson, in a 1929 editorial from the* College Star

In 1971, a new administrative rule mandated that departmental recommendations in regards to promotion and tenure were no longer definitive and that the final arbiter of a candidate's competence and usefulness to the institution would henceforth be "administrative officers." What occurred next is summed up by former Texas State dean of the School of Liberal Arts Ralph H. Houston in *Rosemary for Remembrance: A Memoir* (a discussion of the Southwest Texas State University Department of English on its seventy-fifth anniversary in 1979):

> *The turmoil of the times, accentuated by a recent crisis in top institutional administration* [i.e., McCrocklin], *was almost certainly the background out of which the* [English] *Department was precipitated into a wearying and divisive experience when tenure was denied to three of our staff—Drs. Clyde Grimm, George Pisk and Bill Fowler, all of whom had been recommended* [for tenure] *by the senior staff and chairman.*

Grimm and Pisk received terminal contracts in 1971, and Fowler received his in 1972. Pisk went away quietly, but Grimm and Fowler filed lawsuits against President Jones and the Texas State University System Board of Regents over the loss of their positions on June 15, 1973. In their suits, they charged that they—like John Quincy Adams, Charles Chandler, Allan Butcher, Robert Smith, et al. before them—were fired because of their extracurricular political activity rather than their scholarly work or their academic competence.

In the contemporary coverage of the matter from the *Weather Report*, John Pfeffer commented that, in comparison with Pisk and Grimm, who both had PhDs, President Jones operated at a "freshman level." Dr. Martha Luan Brunson, a professor in the English Department at that time (and for thirty-one years all together—eleven as the English Department chair and fourteen as associate dean of the School of Liberal Arts—she was also awarded the title Distinguished Professor of English Emerita in 1999), would phrase things a little more politely. "[Texas State has] been a training ground for people who go ahead to do other things," Brunson observed. "When [Billy Mac] Jones was here as president, he was a novice at it. He learned how to be a president here, and I think that is unfortunate." President Jones left Texas State in late 1973 to fill the same position at Memphis State University.

At the U.S. Federal Western District Court in Austin, Texas, in mid-December 1974, once again in front of Judge Jack Roberts, President Jones denied that Pisk and Grimm had ever been on a tenure track or offered tenure status. Texas State attorneys then produced the retired vice president of academic affairs, Dr. Joe H. Wilson—the same Joe Wilson who attempted to expropriate the final word on the San Marcos 10 protest in a clearly slanted statement—testified that Grimm had exercised "poor judgment," because he had become inebriated at a party and used "distasteful" four-letter words. The explanation for the termination of Fowler's contract was even more dubious. The administration indicated that Fowler was in the process of receiving a PhD from the University of Texas at the same time that Texas State was charting a new course toward "geographic diversity" in its hiring practices. The university claimed that, because of this new policy, it had become intent on reducing the number of PhD holders it employed from the University of Texas, so the decision was made to terminate Fowler's contract.

It didn't come out at the trial, but two associate professors had joined the Texas State English Department just before the fall semester of 1968. One of these professors was Dr. Grimm, who came from Sam Houston State University in Huntsville but held a PhD from the University of Illinois, and the other was brand-new University of Texas graduate school product Dr. Nancy Grayson. While Fowler was supposedly passed over for his origins in the University of Texas's grad school, Grayson weathered the "geographic" culling and went on to become the English Department chair in the late 1980s.

Grayson said that Fowler had been the faculty sponsor for a Texas State affiliate of the radical antiwar group Students for a Democratic Society at the time and noted that Grimm had a quick wit that often rubbed people the wrong way. She attributed her own staying power to diligence. "My parents taught me to work," she contended. "So that's what I did."

David Bayless doesn't remember Fowler but said he is very familiar with Grimm. He indicated that Grimm actually invited representatives of the San Antonio chapter of the Student Nonviolent Coordinating Committee (SNCC)[79] to speak at Texas State. He also said the participating members hitchhiked and that some showed up with bullet belts strapped diagonally across their chests. He characterized the event as something of a spectacle but insisted that the main speaker was "very articulate" and compelling. Bayless wound up helping the SNCC representatives get home afterward.

Bayless took at least one of Grimm's courses and described him as an outsider. "He sometimes wore sandals with his slacks and tailored shirts," Bayless said. "His classes were exciting and enlightening, what one expected and hoped college would be like."

In a recent interview, Fowler insisted that he was never a faculty sponsor for any progressive student groups but admits he was involved in a controversial but very important chapter of San Marcos politics and education.

On Monday, January 25, 1971, nineteen high school students and four junior high students were suspended from the San Marcos Consolidated Independent School District (SMCISD) for newly instituted dress and grooming violations; another sixty were sent home. The new dress code prohibited sunglasses, T-shirts, hair over the collar or ears (for male students) and sideburns below the ear lobes (for male students). For female students, blue jeans, jumpsuits and pedal pushers were forbidden, and skirt lengths and formfitting outfits were carefully monitored. The son of the former U.S. ambassador to Australia, William Crook, was affected by the suspension, and later that evening, several concerned parents met at the Crook residence and formed a Committee of Concerned Parents to organize an opposition to the new code. The group drafted a letter to the school board and Superintendent Gordon Harmon, requesting that: (1) an investigative committee to reappraise the dress code be created; (2) the school district immediately reinstate the suspended students until the matter was resolved;

and (3) "full assurance be given that no reprisals of any sort be made against a student or employee" involved in the matter.

The school board subsequently held a closed session and reinstated the suspended students until the board reconvened. On January 28, the school board met in special session and voted five to two to uphold the new dress code. Crook's daughter, Elizabeth, now a well-regarded Texas author,[80] shared her thoughts on her family's participation in the crisis in an article titled "Dad vs. the Dress Code" in the August 2004 issue of *Texas Monthly*:

When the dress code went into effect, it was immediately disruptive. Students, who, for years, had gone to school in hand-me-down blue jeans and cheap white T-shirts, were suddenly in trouble when they showed up dressed that way. Black students with afros were sent home. Hispanic high school boys were made to shave their mustaches. Minorities quickly turned against the dress code. Parents started appearing at the schools, demanding to talk to the principals and counselors. Who could afford to dress their kids in shirt collars and coordinated slack-suits? they asked. And who wanted to?

An antiwar poster, circa 1969–73. *Courtesy of the Library of Congress.*

Their questions were all but ignored. Students who didn't comply with the code were sent home or made to wait in the principal's office until someone brought them a change of clothes. They missed exams. Their grades fell. Repeat offenders were suspended.

Students began circulating petitions protesting the "Harmonization." The dress code called for "businesslike" attire, so they appeared in T-shirts with fake ties painted on them. A handful of professors from Southwest Texas State University refused to make their sons cut their hair when they were threatened with suspension. Bob Barton, an activist in town, published editorials against the dress code in his liberal newspaper [the Hays County Free Press].

Within a few months, opposition to the dress code—which affected Mexican American and African American students as much as if not more than their white counterparts—had evolved into a full-throated civil rights campaign, led by local Mexican American leaders and prominent local liberals like William Crook. Frustrations with the dress code and grooming policies were soon exacerbated by other inequities that troubled the Mexican American citizenry. Mexican American children made up 60 percent of the SMCISD enrollment, but there were only a handful of Spanish-speaking personnel working in the school system (one of whom was Juan R. Palomo), and speaking Spanish at all was officially discouraged. In early May, a disparate, mostly Chicano coalition threatened a boycott, and on Cinco de Mayo[81] in 1971, almost half of the SMCISD's 4,655 students participated in the boycott and stayed home from school.

On Wednesday, May 20, Superintendent Harmon and the school board trustees met with eight boycott leaders in a high school conference room to discuss their grievances. The meeting did not go well. Harmon said that "[it was] about time educators [were] left to build an educational program," because "[educators knew] more about [them] than the average lay citizen." Boycott representative and former city councilman Ruben Ruiz was unimpressed. "My people are tired," he said. "I consider this boycott a beginning....If changes are not made, then there will be other boycotts covering the school and the business community."

At the start of the new school year in August, 160 SMCISD students were blocked from attending classes because their garments didn't meet the standards established in the new dress and grooming policies. All but 43 students returned the following day in full compliance. Tensions between the coalition elements and the school board continued to build through that fall semester and climaxed in mid-December. A West German exchange student named Udo Wenz, who was sponsored by the local Rotary Club, was sent home on Tuesday, December 7, because his hair was too long. When he returned to school the following day, unobservant of the policies, he was sent home again. On Saturday, December 11, Ruiz criticized the school's treatment of Wenz and called for Superintendent Harmon's immediate resignation and boycotts of the community's schools and places of business. Wenz got a haircut and returned to school on Monday, December 13. "I am tired of the dress code and all the conversations," he said. "I like this country and do not want to risk the chance of having to leave it."

By late February 1972, the school board agreed to establish a fifty-five-member committee to consider a revision of the district's dress code. A seventh-grade Elizabeth Crook served on the committee, but it went nowhere, and the situation became combative again the following month.

On March 14, 1972, three groups involved with the coalition—including the Mexican American Youth Organization (MAYO), whose Southwest Texas State University chapter was headed up by a junior named Gilbert Ortiz Saenz—delivered a list of grievances to Superintendent Harmon. The grievances included requests for the elimination of the district dress code, the acquisition of Mexican American and African American literature with an area in the school library devoted to this collection, student election reforms, an ethnically balanced student grievance council, the creation of a parental advisory committee, college counseling for black and Chicano students, the establishment of curriculum devoted to Mexican American and African American history, the employment of more black and Chicano teachers and coaches and amnesty for all students who would be participating in the boycott.[82]

On Tuesday, March 21, 1972, after first period, 258 students left their classes and began an indefinite boycott of school. One of the students was Dr. Bill Fowler's daughter, Severra. A petition supporting the boycott was circulated around San Marcos the next day, gaining signatures from Ruiz, former school board trustee Celistino Mendez, prominent members of the liberal Anglo community, a number of Texas State students and Palomo, who was then a co-editor of *La Otra Voz*, a semi-monthly publication devoted to bicultural readers in Hays and the surrounding counties.

By Friday, March 24, there had been 1,200 unexcused absences, and the school board trustees filed a class action lawsuit against progressive school board candidate Phil Waters and thirty-four parents, students and boycott leaders, including Severra Fowler, Palomo, Saenz and future school board member Peter Rodriguez. The suit charged that the parents and students were in violation of compulsory school attendance laws and asked for the recovery of state funds lost through the "inattendance" caused by the boycott, plus $50,000 in exemplary damages. Dr. Fowler and others began to retain lawyers, but on Wednesday, March 29, both sides of the dispute agreed to begin negotiating their differences and cease the boycott. The negotiations were rocky and broke down at one point, but things were eventually hammered out with the assistance of a U.S. Department of Justice mediator. It was in the midst of all this that Dr. Fowler received his terminal contract from Texas State.

When the *Austin American-Statesman* approached a few conservative San Marcos Anglos for their comments on the boycott in early April 1972, their remarks were telling. One conservative observed, "It's that damn group of radical Mexicans at the university that's causing all the trouble." Another said, "You let me run ten, maybe five, people out of town, and I'll solve this whole problem."

In early April 1972, Waters lost his campaign for the school board, but two other progressives—Nancy Hanks Ellis, who had signed an affidavit supporting the San Marcos 10, and Peter Rodriguez—won seats. In mid-April, former *Purgatory Creek Press* editor Bill Cunningham—still enrolled at Texas State—became the first college student in San Marcos to be elected to the city council. Cunningham would soon be joined by the 1965 co-founder of Students' Committee for Professors' Rights (created to defend Bill C. Malone), Eddy Etheridge.

In late July 1972, the school board and the boycott representatives reached an accord (granting the boycotters virtually everything they had asked for), and the board trustees' class action suit was dismissed. In April 1973, Waters won a seat on the school board, where he was joined by another Mexican American community leader, Geronimo "Jerry" Flores.

Though Dr. Fowler referred to himself as a "minor activist, not a leader but a follower" in a recent interview, he said he was a "very enthusiastic follower." He continued to contend that his daughter's participation in the boycott and the resulting lawsuit couldn't have escaped the notice of the remaining conservative elements in the Texas State administration. And he suggested that in whatever capacity he was perceived to be radical, he was naïve and the university was careful not to expose or admit any political or philosophical prejudice during the hearings involving his and Grimm's lawsuit.

Judge Roberts ruled against Grimm and Fowler in January 1975, but Grimm pressed on alone, appealing to the Fifth Circuit Court of Appeals in June 1976. This litigation was also unsuccessful.

———◆———

The story of the San Marcos 10, however, had come full circle. The first curbs of progressive activism at Texas State occurred when instructors John Quincy Adams and Charles Chandler worked with Mexican Americans and African Americans to turn out the minority vote at the 1964 Hays County

Precinct Convention. One of the earliest instances of student activism at Texas State was mounted in 1965, after Bill C. Malone endangered his chances for promotion by participating in civil rights protests in Huntsville. The Texas State student arrested with him was Wayne Oakes, who would later become involved with the ACLU and be on hand at the November 13, 1969 Vietnam Moratorium demonstration at the *Fighting Stallions* statue.

Juan R. Palomo, the Texas State student who came up with the idea for local Vietnam moratorium observations, would later engage the SMCISD as part of a grass-roots, progressive San Marcos coalition, which included Texas State students and faculty members. Nancy Hanks Ellis, a corroborating witness in the San Marcos 10 court battle, would be a part of this coalition and win a SMCISD school board seat to help vanquish some of the stubborn vestiges of conservative repression in the community. Eddy Etheridge, the Texas State alumnus who co-helmed the Students' Committee for Professors' Rights to defend Malone, would be elected to the San Marcos City Council in 1972. Purged *College Star* managing editor (and *Purgatory Creek Press* editor) Bill Cunningham would join Etheridge on the San Marcos City Council while he was still a Texas State student.

From the initial instances of progressive activism in the mid-1960s to those still going on in the early 1970s, everything was connected. Forward-thinking students, professors and citizens contributed to a profound, decade-long struggle that carried the college and the community forward and made the city of San Marcos and Texas State University what they are today—better places to live and learn.

Dr. Fowler wound up at Iowa State University, where he taught until his retirement in 1992. Then, he got a law degree and began practicing in San Antonio. Palomo would go on to write for the *Houston Post*, the *Austin American-Statesman* and *USA Today*. Eddy Etheridge became the mayor of San Marcos and later served as a Hays County judge. Bill Cunningham went on to serve as a legislative aide for U.S. representative J.J. Pickle and would later become the chair of the Texas State University System Board of Regents. A San Marcos icon, Cunningham passed away on April 19, 2018.

MARTINE'S SCAM

*We could see in our own country as late as the 1960's and 1970's how good
Christian and Jewish men, the pillars of our society, when they acceded to
political and military power, could sit calmly and coolly in their air-conditioned
offices in Washington and cold-bloodedly, without a qualm or a moral quiver,
plan and order the massacre of hundreds of thousands of men, women and
children and the destruction of their homes, farms, churches, schools and hospitals
in a faraway Asian land of poor peasants who had never threatened us in the
slightest, who were incapable of it. Almost as savage was the acceptance by most
of us citizens of such barbarism, until, toward the end, our slumbering—or
should one say, cowardly?—consciences were aroused.*
—William L. Shirer, American journalist, author and war correspondent

I n late October 2001, the San Marcos 10 were invited back to Texas
State University to participate in a day-long forum on free speech
and other First Amendment freedoms. The event was planned well
before 9/11 (which had occurred the month before), and it included a
conversation with famed *Austin American-Statesman* editorial cartoonist Ben
Sargent, a roundtable with *Austin American-Statesman* editor Rich Oppel and
San Antonio Express-News editor Robert Rivard, a presentation by former
CIA agent Frank Shepp and a panel discussion with the seven members of
the San Marcos 10 who were in attendance.

During the San Marcos 10 forum, members of the infamous group
were heartened by the nostalgia surrounding their historical stance and

San Marcos 10 protester David Bayless (*front row, fifth from the left*) lettered in baseball at Texas State before he left for Vietnam. He returned to school in 1969. *From the 1964* Pedagog *yearbook.*

discussed it with an undiminished sense of defiance and pride. Mike Holman, then fifty-five years old, indicated that he had basically stood up for something he believed in. "I still think we were right," he said. David Bayless, then sixty years old, claimed he'd do things differently if given the chance. "I'd be louder," he observed. "I would do even more. There's no question." Annie Burleson, then fifty-one years old, recalled the fear she felt in the pit of her stomach as she and the others waited for Dean Martine to return, but she also said that she had no regrets. "I needed to stay," she said. "I felt I had the right to be there."

At one inauspicious moment during the proceedings, Martine himself—who was not a designated panel guest or speaker—grabbed the microphone and (for what he, no doubt, considered proper measure) began sharing the university's position at the time and engaged in further attempts to "dean-splain." He said, "The protesters were not causing a disturbance, but we had about two hundred rednecks around who wanted to run them out of town." Cited in newspaper reports as having retired from the university in 1975, Martine insisted that the problem with the protest wasn't the participants' antiwar stance but that he had told them to leave. "If you don't want to follow the rules, you're not our enemy," he said. "But if we send you home, don't cry. These rules and regulations were gone over by everybody. It wasn't something hastily put together."

What happened next was perhaps the most important moment of the symposium.

Frustrated that Martine had practically commandeered the microphone and inserted himself into the dialogue, Sallie Ann Satagaj reestablished the entire point of the discussion. "Some things never change," she said. "I'm not going to sit and listen to you give me another three minutes. I'm going to try to be kind—but you were wrong, you were wrong, *you were wrong*. It's not free expression if you tell me where I can stand and what time I can be there. We were silent, we were right. We're right today."

In the end, the San Marcos 10 panel discussion was civil and often jovial where Martine was concerned. In fact, some members of the 10 had already buried the hatchet with Martine and were friendly. At the original November 13, 1969 protest, Martine had confiscated the 10's student IDs; when the 10's twenty-year reunion was held in 1989,[83] Martine reportedly returned the confiscated student IDs to them. Floyd Martine succumbed to cancer at the age of eighty on February 11, 2004. The accomplishments listed in his obituary were stated plainly: "His lifelong career in Texas education included being a coach a Fulmore Jr. High [Austin], a counselor at Travis High [Austin] and Dean of Students at (SWT) Texas State University."

In 2001, the *Austin American-Statesman*'s coverage of the free speech event at Texas State characterized Martine as modest about his place in the school's history, and coupled with his short, unassuming obituary, one might get the impression that he was just a humble educator, and that he and the San Marcos 10 had simply (and unfortunately) been on opposite sides of a technicality. This narrative certainly played well for Texas State in 2001, but—intentional or no—it was a bald-faced fiction. Martine's issue with the San Marcos 10 involved much more than a technicality, and he didn't retire from the university in 1975 (as the *Statesman* indicated)—he resigned in disgrace.

———— ◆ ————

The last noteworthy stand Dean Martine made as an employee of Texas State involved a coed and a goldfish—and he was unceremoniously drubbed.

In the early 1970s, it was mandatory for young women who attended Texas State to join the Association of Women Students (AWS). The AWS was a rigid, authoritarian entity funded by mandatory membership fees, and one of its pet peeves was pets in dormitory rooms. They were strictly forbidden. In early November 1974, Texas State student Tonia Gayle Moreno was caught with a goldfish in her dormitory room after an unscheduled search. She received "campus restriction" for two weekends but subsequently challenged the punishment. Fellow Texas State student Charles Sims assisted Moreno in her defense, claiming that the university (1) performed an illegal search; (2) forced female students to join AWS and therefore its rules were invalid; (3) provided no adequate recourse to the requirements established by the undemocratic organization; (4) forced female students to pay an illegal fee to support AWS; (5) denied Moreno due process; (6) imposed a punitive measure it had no authority to enforce; and (7) discriminated against Moreno because of her gender.

Dean Martine was present when the case was brought before the Students Rights Committee of the Associated Student Government; but instead of chiding Moreno, the committee members rejected the administration's position and recommended censure for Dean Martine "for unwarranted and excessive action."

The issue was brought to the attention of Texas attorney general John Hill when Dean Martine pushed for a formal, outside opinion on the matter. The attorney general's office declined to address the situation, and Assistant Attorney General Bill Bednar instructed Martine to contact the State Coordinating Board for the Texas College and University System for assistance. Martine chose not to contact the State Coordinating Board and instead reduced Moreno's punishment to a zero-tolerance probationary period.

Adding insult to Dean Martine's injury, one of the main editorials in the April 4, 1975 edition of the *University Star* deplored "the inflexibility and lack of judgment demonstrated by the Dean of Students" and concluded with a bold request:

> *The* Star *urges the establishment of an atmosphere where students are free to express their views, petition for their rights and appeal university decisions without being subjected to the disciplinary whims of the Dean of Students Office.*

Less than four weeks later, Martine abruptly faced a much deeper and more serious calamity, scrambling to explain the findings of an audit rather than an illegal search.

In late April, a state auditor discovered irregularities in the Dean of Students Office's management of the premiums of a Blue Cross Blue Shield

Student Health Plan. Martine had arrived at Texas State in 1959 and became the dean of students in 1967; not long after his promotion and continuing until the discrepancies were discovered in early April 1975, Martine had intermittently withdrawn large personal sums from the insurance fund. He explained that the monies had been used to repay a farm equipment loan, and he repaid the funds with interest every time he borrowed. However, there were also large "disbursements for operating expenses" that had not been sufficiently documented. Texas State president Lee H. Smith stated: "Unless proper support is provided for these disbursements, the university and the state auditors will seek restitution for the full amount plus interest."

Editorial cartoon featuring Dean Floyd Martine and acting university president Leland Derrick presiding over "The Friendly Campus on the Hill" in the December 1, 1970 issue of the *Weather Report. Courtesy of the Wittliff Collections, Albert B. Alkek Library at Texas State University.*

Under the circumstances, President Smith asked for and received Martine's resignation, expressing sincere regret. "Martine has served well the needs of the many students at SWT," Smith observed. "And he has many friends and supporters." When asked about the prosecution of the former dean, President Smith was sympathetic. "In view of his long years of service to the institution," Smith said, "and in keeping with his expressed willingness to work with state auditors and the institution…the university has elected not to file criminal charges at this time." The special consideration Martine received would come back to haunt Texas State.

The date of Martine's resignation was incredibly coincidental, fateful and/or karmic. It occurred on April 28, 1975—the same day America's involvement in Vietnam came to an end.

By early June 1975, Martine had not made restitution for the disputed funds he resigned over. A Hays County grand jury that included four Texas State professors (Dr. Randall Bland,[84] assistant professor of political science; Dr. Walter Corrie, sociology professor; Dr. Ted Keck, chairman of the Health and Physical Education Department; and Gerald Champagne, associate professor of agriculture) subsequently instituted an examination of the matter without formal complaint from law enforcement personnel or private citizens. On Wednesday, June 4, 1975, Hays County jurors gave Martine an ultimatum, stating that if full restitution was not made to the university by September 1, 1975, the next grand jury would consider prosecution.

———

A few years after his resignation, Martine, who was working as an administrator of an Austin retirement home at the time, decided to sue Texas State and the Texas State University System Board of Regents (which had charitably accepted and approved the resignation rather than terminating him outright) over what he was terming as his "firing." Originally, he had resigned for "moral turpitude and gross neglect of duties." But since the university had neglected to prosecute him, he initiated litigation claiming that the allegations against him had not been proven and that the insurance fund he had been borrowing from was moved off-campus and, therefore, should have been viewed as a private endeavor. Essentially, Martine claimed that, as a tenured employee, his employment could not have been terminated without demonstrable cause, and the former dean of students was seeking full retirement benefits, lost wages and damages.

In 1979, District Court judge Hume Cofer reversed what was then being referred to as the Texas State University System Board of Regents' "firing" of Martine. The Board of Regents appealed the ruling to the Third Court of Civil Appeals. Ultimately, the appellate court agreed with the district court ruling and ordered Martine be reinstated in October 1980.

On January 2, 1981, the Texas State University System Board of Regents asked the Texas Supreme Court to overturn the Third Court of Civil Appeals' decision. Texas State University lawyer William Fly then convincingly argued that Martine's repeated, unauthorized removal of funds ($103,500 altogether) constituted "misconduct" and that his breach of responsibility and trust was clearly "connected with his profession as a member of the administration and faculty" of the university. Despite this argument, on February 25, 1981, the Texas Supreme Court ruled that there had been no reversible error by the lower courts. In late fall 1981, the Sixty-Seventh Legislature of the State of Texas approved an employment settlement for Martine and paid him forthwith. The sum Martine received was the same amount the San Marcos 10 had been denied: $100,000.[85]

When the *Austin American-Statesman* failed to give the Martine settlement the attention his supporters believed it deserved, the "Friends of Floyd Martine" purchased a boxed news advertisement titled "Justice—At Last." It ran in the *Statesman* on November 1, 1981:

> *After six long years, the case involving Dean Floyd Martine and Southwest Texas State University has been settled.*
>
> *SWTU has agreed to pay Dean Martine all back salary and retirement benefits resulting from his unjust termination by Dr. Lee H. Smith in 1975.*
>
> *Dean Martine won his case in the 98th Judicial Court, the Third Court of Civil Appeals and the Supreme Court of the State of Texas. Each [sic] of those courts ruled that the SWTU administration and the Board of Regents terminated Dean Martine without just cause.*
>
> *With his reinstatement, ordered by the courts, Dean Martine is eligible to, and will, retire on full benefits.*
>
> *Those of us who know him are delighted that this educator would not bow down under pressure…would not accept the intimidations of a huge bureaucracy…would not give up the fight to prove his case.*
>
> *We deeply regret the public embarrassment suffered by his family.*

We also regret that the SWTU administration repeatedly tried to deny Dean Martine his rights of appeal of the board's decision. Hopefully, future administrators will learn from this case.

We slaute [sic] *Dean Martine and hope he will visit his many friends on the SWTU campus often.*

———

When I originally spoke with Sidney Lupu in late November 2018, he relayed the details of his participation in the October 15, 1969 Vietnam Moratorium and Martine's warning. Then, he told me about how ridiculous the crowd's response to the demonstration had been. At the time, I didn't press him about what he meant, but when I went through the interview notes later, I realized I might have missed something. So, I got back in touch with Lupu and revisited the subject.

"It *was* ridiculous," he maintained.

"How so?" I asked.

"It wouldn't have been a big deal," he said. "Just a bunch of antiwar students sitting around a statue. But the…the…*I don't know what to call them.*"

"The cowboys and jocks?"

"Yes," Lupu said. "Yes. They *made* it a big deal."

It goes without saying that 1969 was a trying year for Texas State, and it could be argued that Martine et al. clamped down on the San Marcos 10 because the university didn't need any more bad press, but that's exactly what the San Marcos 10 became. And Martine's problem with students harboring antiwar leanings started well before November 13.

Martine had no problem with pro-war students confronting a few of their antiwar classmates and burning permitted antiwar literature in 1967. The obverse certainly wouldn't have been accepted or tolerated. Martine also expressed no issue with a distributor of said literature getting roughed up by pro-war elements (at the time, Martine plainly and dismissively stated that the majority of the Texas State student body was simply not "sympathetic" to the antiwar cause). Again, the obverse certainly wouldn't have been accepted or tolerated. Martine also, apparently, had no problem with pro-war students joking about tossing their antiwar classmates into a bonfire. Not only would the obverse not have been tolerated, it may have led to suspensions. Consider then, if you will, the earlier mentioned clean-cut, "anti-protest" student depicted handing out pro-war leaflets on the front page of the December 10, 1965 *College Star*. Does anyone really believe Martine or the administration would have ignored a large group of antiwar students assaulting him or placing all of his leaflets in a pile and burning them on the steps of the Student Center?

Then, when Martin Luther King mourner Vernon Edwards barricaded Old Main in 1968, Martine applied a "dash of sugar" instead of a "barrel of vinegar." Edwards and the others were knowingly and willfully disruptive, but Martine issued no three-minutes-to-disperse ultimatums and zero you're-finished-at-this-university threats. What happened to the student expression rules that day? Was there too much visibility after King's assassination? Was the unauthorized barricade too spontaneous?

At the larger, first prohibited, then permitted, anti-McCrocklin protest on February 20, 1969—nine months before the San Marcos 10 suspension—Martine actually held an umbrella over some of the protesters' heads and let the demonstration carry on well past the designated student expression midday time slot. Was he still on the sugar over vinegar kick, or was he playing nice because the university had already written McCrocklin off?

Al Henson back at the base of the *Fighting Stallions* statue at Texas State in 2001. *Courtesy of the* Austin American-Statesman.

When fifty students held a study-in protesting the termination of four instructors associated with the McCrocklin resignation in May 1969—just six months prior to the San Marcos 10 suspensions—local media outlets covering the demonstration noted that the protesters were clearly violating the student expression rules. Where was Martine? Where were the administrative ultimatums?

During the San Marcos 10 portion of the First Amendment Freedoms Forum in October 2001, Martine claimed that politics played no role in the 10's suspensions. "If you don't follow the rules, you're not our enemy," he said. "But if we send you home, don't cry."

Did the San Marcos 10 deserve to be sent home more than Cliff Berkman in 1967?

Did the San Marcos 10 deserve to be dismissed more than the students who barricaded Old Main in 1968?

Did the San Marcos 10 deserve to be punished any more than the earlier student expression rule-defying "McCrocklin flu" demonstrators in May 1969?

What about when Martine practically had to restrain an over-animated pro-war heckler at the October 15, 1969 Vietnam Moratorium demonstration? There's no evidence the disruptive pro-war student was ever warned or cautioned at all, but Martine had no qualms over threatening Lupu for peaceably speaking up for the antiwar protesters. That's the main reason Lupu thought the hostility toward the first Texas State Vietnam Moratorium observance was "ridiculous"—he suspected that some of it was staged. Many of the cowboys and jocks may have shown up of their own accord, but it seemed to Lupu that a considerable percentage of the pro-war onlookers behaved more like goons sent by the administration.

Is it possible that Martine and Texas State administrators planned for the October 15 demonstration to end with a whimper and perhaps another "SWT Rejects Peaceniks" headline?

Is it possible that Martine and Texas State administrators underestimated the amount of antiwar sentiment on campus and that the threats against students like Lupu, faculty members who allowed students to attend the moratorium and counselors and student housing personnel who refused to report on protesting students were simply damage control measures made in an attempt to regain the upper hand?

These speculations certainly explain the urgency to mitigate or obstruct the effectiveness of the November 13, 1969 Moratorium.

And it gets worse.

When Juan R. Palomo lived on Texas State's campus, he made the acquaintance of a conservative cowboy who later enjoyed boasting about his involvement in the intimidation of antiwar demonstrators during the

Vietnam moratoriums in late 1969. In fact, this pro-war student claimed Texas State administrators put him and others like him up to it. He said he was proud of what he had done and told Palomo as much. Down the road, however, this cowboy's position on the war changed. And when he ran into Palomo years later, he was ashamed. He even asked Palomo to forgive him.[86]

The incident is notable, because it resembles other mentions of such machinations. The administration also reportedly sent football players to "shout down" anti-McCrocklin sentiment at the December 17, 1968 plagiarism forum.

———◆———

On the morning of November 13, 1969, Dr. Richard B. Henderson was up in one of the buildings next to the *Fighting Stallions* statue, just above the San Marcos 10 protest. He said, at the time, that the antiwar demonstrators were not disruptive and indicated that it was the surrounding crowd that was the problem. Later, in an October 17, 1985 interview with Texas State student Stephany S. Goodbread, Henderson remarked that he thought "the students had the better case" but that the university had prevailed through "subterfuge."

Looking back, this assessment is hardly debatable.

The fall semester of 1969 was the first semester (or first semester back)[87] at Texas State for half of the San Marcos 10, and the rest hadn't been present at or very familiar with the 1967 antiwar pamphlet bonfire, the 1968 MLK assassination barricade, the April 1969 removal of a Vietnam War–themed piece of artwork, the McCrocklin protest, etc. These students certainly didn't have access to the instant internet database recall that we enjoy today, so when ACLU lawyers put together the 10's defense, they were unaware of a number of exculpatory facts. After recently learning more about the background of the university's stance on antiwar activism in that era, former attorney Mark Levbarg was frustrated. "I was specifically asked by Judge Roberts if the administration had shown any animus toward the students' ideas," Levbarg said. "Had I known [about the other events on campus], I would have insisted animus was shown. I would have demonstrated animus was shown, and I would have gotten them [the San Marcos 10] off."

The Fifth Circuit Court's review of Judge Roberts's findings determined that Texas State's suspension of the San Marcos 10 was "a valid exercise of the University's right to adopt and enforce reasonable, non-discriminatory regulation as to time, place and manner of student expressions and demonstrations." If animus had been demonstrated by the 10's defense, Texas State's argument would have fallen apart, because its attempt at regulation would clearly have been deemed discriminatory. As in the case later brought by Clyde Grimm and Bill Fowler, however, the university "was careful not to expose or admit any political or philosophical prejudice during the hearings." And Texas State apparently got one over on U.S. jurisprudence in both matters.

Martine's lack of recall on the subject during the October 2001 First Amendment forum was either a convenient lapse in memory or a self-serving lie. He and the Texas State administration had to have been aware of their arbitrary utilization of the student expression rules, and therein lay the subterfuge.

14

CIVIL OBEDIENCE

*Civil disobedience is not our problem. Our problem is civil obedience. Our problem
is that people all over the world have obeyed the dictates of leaders…and millions
have been killed because of this obedience.…Our problem is that people are
obedient all over the world in the face of poverty and starvation and stupidity, and
war, and cruelty.*
—*Howard Zinn, author of* The People's History of the United States

Today, San Marcos 10 witness and former SMCISD school board
trustee Nancy Hanks Ellis says that what she remembers most about
the San Marcos 10 was how impressive and "dignified" they seemed
while sitting peacefully at the base of the *Fighting Stallions* statue on November
13, 1969. The photographic record of the demonstration supports this
observation; the 10's dignity was apparent. But that didn't sway Texas State
administrators.

After the San Marcos 10 were suspended, Frances Vykoukal wrote a
letter to her Sealy High School government teacher, Billy Preibisch. Sealy
was a conservative town, and Mrs. Preibisch had taught at the high school
for a long time. Vykoukal's father had even been one of her pupils. In the
letter, Frances expressed how much she appreciated what she had learned
in Preibisch's class and that she had been putting that knowledge to work
at Texas State. Vykoukal said that even though the basic principles of those
lessons were now getting her kicked out of school, she still believed in the
right to free speech in America. Preibisch attempted to read the letter to one
of her classes but broke down in tears.

Former Texas State student Eddy Etheridge and current student Bill Cunningham being sworn in for their seats on the San Marcos City Council in April 1972. *From the 1973* Pedagog *yearbook.*

The chief problem that critics of the antiwar movement faced was not that the demonstrators were unfamiliar with or ignoring American ideals; the problem was that too many of the protesters had been raised with these ideals and knew them by heart. In the final decade of the last half-century, it has been widely, roundly and authoritatively established that America's war in Vietnam[88] was shockingly wrongheaded, monumentally ill-advised and, when beheld in perspective on the grand canvas of United States history, comprised a singular evil. "Pentagon Papers" source Daniel Ellsberg put it best at the time: "We're not on the wrong side. We are the wrong side."

It's a sobering revelation and one that requires a diligent approach to accountability and responsibility going forward—but also looking back. The Nixon and Johnson administrations' greatest challenge was to convince Americans who were actually paying attention and knew better that they did *not* know better.

Because many actually did.

At the time, a large portion of our country may not have recognized what was happening in Vietnam or effectively grasped the reasons and motives behind the war. It had only been a generation since World War II, and the American people still granted their government a deference that politicians counted on and certainly took advantage of. But in places like the American university, where an anonymous Texas State faculty member correctly pointed out that doubt should be "the essence of all philosophical and scientific endeavors" and skepticism a part of education, many instructors and professors were doing their jobs and encouraging students to reason independently. And many students were learning to think for themselves and question the status quo.

———◆———

In *The Big Lebowski*, aging hippie stoner Jeff "The Dude" Lebowski mentions that he was one of the authors of the original *Port Huron Statement*[89] and a member of the "Seattle Seven."[90] While this entertaining portrayal of a fifty-something-year-old 1960s radical is engaging and fun, it is just a pleasant caricature of the real thing. There were no Jeff Lebowskis in the San Marcos 10.

Rosenwasser did open a headshop called Happy Trails in San Marcos, but he also worked in real estate and imports and remained active in local politics. Holman went to work for the State Comptroller's Office. Satagaj graduated from Texas State and became a librarian in the Austin Public Library system. She remains a social activist and still participates in protests today. Saranello received a law degree from the University of Texas, worked as an attorney in Houston and now does insurance consulting in Colorado. After several stints as a piano technician, Burleson, like McConchie, became a nurse. Cates finished his degree at Texas State and spent his career teaching history at Kennedy High School and Rhodes Middle School in San Antonio. After touring around the country in rock bands for a while, Henson started working in entertainment booking and stayed in the music business for another forty years. Bayless finished his degree at Texas State and went on to work with troubled youths and the mentally ill.

In retrospect, the remaining members of the San Marcos 10 view their involvement in the November 13, 1969 Vietnam Moratorium philosophically.

"I have never regretted it in the slightest degree," said Cates. "I've always been very, very proud that I stayed for the demonstration. I feel like it was one of the most important things I've done in my life."

"Things had reached critical mass," Rosenwasser observed. "People were getting killed, and I knew what was going on. I knew all the arguments. I knew we [the 10] were on the right track. It was a real cultural revolution, the kind of thing that only happens every hundred years or so."

"It all changed with the Kennedy assassination," Holman said. "I can't tell you exactly when I woke up, but I did. It was probably brought on by the behavior of our government. I wasn't angry. It's not like I hated my country, and I didn't hate our soldiers. But our government—what it was up to, it wasn't American. I couldn't abide by it. I couldn't stand by it."

"Still, today," Henson maintained, "no one can give a good reason—that makes sense, at least—why we were in Vietnam."

"I gave up my whole college career because of the war," Henson said. "At the time, I thought it was a crushing blow, but it was just another turn in the road. I stood up for what I thought was right, and I wouldn't trade any of it for anything."

"There have been people all through history who were willing to stand up to the tanks in Tiananmen Square, to the Nazis and to tyrannical governments and regimes of every kind," Satagaj said. "To say 'don't do this to the Rohingya.' There has to be somebody who has a social consciousness, and if we were some of those people at that time, I am happy to have served that purpose. And I hope that there are those who will follow in our footsteps and play their part in whatever comes next."

"We had some First Amendment rights on our side, but we knew there was no guarantee," remembered Saranello. "By 1969–70, the entire country was mobilizing against the war because people weren't buying the story that the Vietnam War was a fight to save America or save democracy around the world. We felt strongly enough about it to ignore Martine's threats—and we did. And I've never regretted that action."

"My participation in the protest and what came after really opened my eyes," said Burleson. "I'd really been sheltered. I feel like I grew up a lot and started to think more for myself. I remember thinking—*realizing*—that all the history that I'd been taught up to that point was all nice and whitewashed, that there was more to it than what we'd been brought up to believe."

"When I came back from Vietnam," said Bayless, "I had problems talking about it without crying. It's something that stayed with me. You come home, the plane lands, you feel guilty. Guilty for coming back. Guilty for living. It was pretty common. So, this was all a pretty powerful thing, and having a hand in ending it, actually making a statement and making people aware—it was really important to me."

The average American may not have been able to recognize, accept or acknowledge the Vietnam War for what it was, but a handful of young people did. And across the nation, they were separately and variously persecuted, punished and sometimes even shot down for it. The San Marcos 10 were part of this tradition. Two of them were veterans, two of them had military fathers involved in Vietnam and most of the rest had friends or relatives fighting in the conflict. Their dissent was well-reasoned and their principles were sound, but when their own university disparaged their efforts and suspended them for conducting themselves as if they were rational, educated citizens, and when their nation's court system failed them, the 10's chief missteps were having faith in American ideals and assuming enough of their fellow citizens did as well.

—⚬—

On November 13, 1969, ten Texas State students were suspended for excercising free speech at the base of the *Fighting Stallions*. Fifty years later, the *Fighting Stallions* statue—today located a little farther west on the Quad than it was in 1969 and surrounded by concrete instead of grass—is a designated free speech area at the university.

Ironic, yes. But it is also a high compliment (and possibly unwitting acknowledgement), even if somewhat backhanded.

In his diary of the Vietnam War period, President Nixon lamented that American youth "don't know what to do with their lives." The San Marcos 10 knew exactly what to do with their lives, and they shouldn't have lost the credits they earned during the the 1969–70 school year. They didn't fail Texas State University—Texas State University failed them. The San Marcos 10 should be recognized as the champions they were and the champions they remain.

15

POSTSCRIPT

The slow-rising central horror of "Watergate" is not that it might grind down to the reluctant impeachment of a vengeful thug of a president, whose entire political career has been a monument to the same kind of cheap shots and treachery he finally got nailed for, but that we might somehow fail to learn something from it.
—*Hunter S. Thompson,* Rolling Stone, *August 2, 1973*

In early 2003, Sallie Ann Satagaj took part in an antiwar demonstration against the Iraq War just down the road from President George W. Bush's Crawford Ranch. Shortly into the protest, security personnel came out and ordered the protesters to leave. The protesters were informed that they would be given three minutes to disperse. "I thought it was so funny," Satagaj said. "Almost the exact same thing was happening again. I couldn't stop laughing."

Satagaj and the other members of the San Marcos 10 who remained at Texas State went into the summer of 1970 still unsure of their future, but thanks to the Fifth Circuit Court injunction, they had successfully completed another semester of college. The nationwide Vietnam moratoriums of late 1969 had been wildly successful, and the public's opinion of Nixon and the Vietnam War had begun to fluctuate in ways that made the administration uncomfortable. The problem again, however, was that Nixon wasn't doing what he promised: getting the nation out of Vietnam. His charade was complicated by the Kent State shootings, etc., but a new media advisor helped Nixon weather the storm and win reelection in 1972. His name was Roger Ailes.

The Vietnam War was called the first "TV war," and proponents of the U.S. military-industrial complex felt the coverage it received hurt the war effort and recorded this lesson for future military campaigns. *Library of Congress, Prints and Photographs Division.*

For Ailes and the Nixon White House, the problem was never what Nixon was doing wrong or the promises he refused to deliver on. Their problem was that what he was doing was being reported by the American media. And during the course of the summer of 1970, a memo titled "A Plan for Putting the GOP on the News" was circulated. The memo was discovered by John Cook at Gawker in 2011. The following is a telling excerpt:

> *Today, television news is watched more often than people read newspapers, than people listen to the radio, than people read or gather any other form of communication. The reason: People are lazy. With television you just sit—watch—listen. The thinking is done for you.*

Though it isn't clear who originally authored the memo, Ailes's handwritten notes are all over it. The memo also outlined a plan between the Nixon administration and Ailes to coordinate the dissemination of pro-administration news to television networks around the country.

Long before Ailes became a chairman and CEO of Fox News and Fox Television Stations, his acknowledged difficulty with the American media was not that it was too liberal, that it couldn't be trusted or that it was "lamestream"—it was simply that journalists were doing their jobs and reporting the Nixon administration's general failings and contemptible methods. Nixon staffers, like Ailes, considered Nixon's unscrupulous tactics irrelevant—they were only concerned with the American public's perception of their unscrupulousness.

The Vietnam War was considered the first "TV war," and both Johnson and Nixon claimed that TV coverage hurt the American military effort. The images of the dead and wounded soldiers that were aired during the Johnson and Nixon administrations were disturbing and demoralizing. And the images of the antiwar protests and the assault and murder of antiwar protesters during the Nixon administration were unequivocally damning, in the same way that images of the beatings of civil rights protesters had been in the previous decade.

Ailes essentially proposed a "GOP TV" strategy, and though it took twenty years and the repeal of the Fairness Doctrine to get, once Ailes and Fox News achieved it, America changed. If broad swathes of the provincial U.S. citizenry didn't like what responsible journalists were reporting, they had a friend they could turn to, a "news" source that would filter out unwanted criticism, promote conventional perspectives, encourage tacit consent (and conformity) and limit and censor authentic news sources that challenged complacency and established mores. Witch hunts could be perpetrated and never seriously condemned. Wars predicated on outright prevarications could be waged. Journalism hazardous to staid principles and prescribed dogma could be mitigated. TV that portrayed war efforts in unflattering lights could be mitigated. A viewership that knew why or knew better could be mitigated. Ailes's successful incarnation of GOP TV changed everything, even eventually wooing many aging 1960s antiwar protesters—who had previously despised almost everything about Nixonian machinations—into the fold.

The undeniable genius of Roger Ailes was that he knew then what we're finding out now: *If Fox News had been around in the early 1970s, the war in Vietnam would not have ended, the Nixon presidency would not have been mortally wounded by the Watergate Scandal and Nixon himself wouldn't have been forced to resign in disgrace.*

The San Marcos 10 contributed to ending the war in Vietnam, but the folks who supported the war in the Nixon White House—which also included, lest we forget, Donald Rumsfeld and Dick Cheney—took the lessons they learned to heart and returned with a well-coordinated, long-term vengeance (with many of their former foes in tow). With Ailes in the background, Rumsfeld and Cheney went on to be a part of the Ford administration. Then, Ailes advised Ronald Reagan and George H.W. Bush before Rumsfeld and Cheney converged again in the George W. Bush administration. At that point, Ailes was in the foreground via Fox "GOP TV" News, which was unquestionably doing the "thinking" for its viewers and creating another Vietnam—*a stateless Vietnam*—thereby finally perfecting endless conflict. Which has been endlessly profitable for the principals behind American wars for the last half century.

Ailes's final achievement?

Donald J. Trump.

The San Marcos 10 and their contemporaries helped stop a war, end an obscenity and expose a catalogue of abominable lies. But the lies, obscenities and wars still go on, and the most recent proverbial political pendulum swing has been particularly destructive, because the conservative powers that exist today seem to wield the same control that Texas State administrators enjoyed in the late 1960s: a diminished press and the ability to mitigate, if not stifle, dissent.

It's distressing and unfortunate that so many enlightened baby boomers forgot their hula hoops (or put them down), because no generation since has bothered to pick them up. And this is frightening.

Texas State has moved in the right direction. The country as a whole has not.

NOTES

Chapter 1

1. The song can also be heard in season three of HBO's *True Detective* (2019).
2. Up until the new millennium, the *Fighting Stallions* statue was known as the Huntington Mustangs statue. In 1969, the seventeen-foot-high sculpture was located in a patch of grass east of where it sits now.
3. The My Lai Massacre was a mass murder of unarmed South Vietnamese civilians by U.S. troops in the Sơn Tịnh District of South Vietnam on March 16, 1968. Between 350 and 500 unarmed civilians were killed by U.S. soldiers from Company C, First Battalion, Twentieth Infantry Regiment, Eleventh Brigade, Twenty-Third Infantry Division. Victims included men, women, children and infants. Some of the women and young girls were gang-raped.
4. To date, the audio recording of this exchange has never been recovered.
5. Students at the University of Houston did the same thing on a different day.

Chapter 2

6. Wells, *The War Within: America's Battle over Vietnam*, 316.
7. Ibid.
8. Kissinger, *White House Years*, 510.
9. Wells, *The War Within: America's Battle over Vietnam*, 307.

10. Ibid., 351.

11. The second, of course, being Ronald Reagan's last-minute deal with Iran to delay the release of the American hostages just before the 1980 presidential election. Reagan's handlers were afraid a release of the hostages might earn the incumbent president, Jimmy Carter, enough votes to win reelection.

12. "Whitmanesque" is indicative of the broad and optimistic outlook on life that the nineteenth-century American poet, essayist and journalist Walt Whitman demonstrated in his writing.

Chapter 3

13. Juan R. Palomo was born into a migrant, farm-working family in North Dakota. He grew up in south Texas and several Midwestern states. He received a bachelor's degree in art education from Texas State and a master's degree in journalism from American University. He went on to write for several major newspapers and, today, focuses on poetry.

14. Established by the Newman Club (an on-campus Catholic organization) and the Christian Campus Community (made up of mostly Methodists and Presbyterians), the Coffee House was a facility where religious students (of all faiths) and non-religious students could hang out, share ideas, debate issues and mingle. The informal meeting place had no chairs, coffee was sold in the back room and students could sit on the carpeted floor. It was a visionary setting that often hosted on- and off-campus musicians, poets, activists and controversial discussions. Terry McCabe was the director from 1968 to 1969.

15. Though Bob Dylan denied it was a protest song when he first sang it at Gerdes Folk City in Greenwich Village in 1962 (the year before it was officially released), "Blowin' in the Wind" became one of the greatest protest songs of all time.

16. Though titled "Abraham, Martin, John," the 1968 song (first recorded by Dion) includes mention of Robert F. Kennedy and was written after his assassination in June and the assassination of Martin Luther King Jr. in April.

17. A false dilemma is a type of informal fallacy in which something is falsely claimed to be an "either/or" situation when, in fact, there is at least one other option. A false dilemma is often introduced intentionally in an attempt to force a choice or outcome.

Chapter 4

18. Mary Alice Kiker went on to be an attorney and worked on prison reform issues in Texas before moving and practicing law in California.
19. Sidney Lupu is now a schoolteacher in Clark County, Nevada.

Chapter 5

20. Wayne Oakes would go on to become a strong supporter of the Central Texas ACLU and was actually present for the San Marcos 10 protest on November 13, 1969.
21. According to Robert Perkinson, author of *Texas Tough: The Rise of America's Prison Empire*, the Gatesville State School for Boys had "a reputation for ruthlessness." Solitary confinement abuses, stoop labor, violence between gangs, beatings perpetrated by staff members and incidents of sexual assault were reported at the facility before it finally closed in 1979.
22. The earliest act of student activism at Texas State University may have involved its most famous alumnus, Lyndon Baines Johnson. For most of the 1920s, a secret fraternal group known as the "Black Stars" (composed mainly of Beta Sigma athletes) enjoyed a stranglehold on student politics, student publications and student jobs at the school. In 1929, Johnson and eight other students formed a separate group known as the "White Stars" to supplant their entrenched counterparts and did so in remarkably short order.
23. The actual press run of Private First Class George Kreiner's *Marine's Vietnam Diary* was in 1967, and this excerpt appeared in the September 30, 1967 edition of *The Record*. Kreiner (November 22, 1936–August 3, 2012) was from West Paterson, New Jersey.
24. Porter Sparkman would go to work for the *San Antonio Express* after college before pursuing a career in Information Technology.
25. This paraphrasing originates from the fourth paragraph of President Lincoln's November 19, 1863 Gettysburg Address: "But, in a larger sense, we cannot dedicate…we cannot consecrate…we cannot hallow this ground. The brave men, living and dead, who struggled here have consecrated it, far above our poor power to add or detract. The world will little note, nor long remember, what we say here, but it can never forget what they did here."

26. This partial quote actually comes from seventeenth-century English theologian and historian Thomas Fuller. The full quote is: "Fools names and fools faces often appear in public places."
27. Fort Polk is a U.S. Army installation located approximately ten miles east of Leesville, Louisiana, in the Vernon Parish.
28. Camp Pendleton is the major West Coast base of the United States Marine Corps. It is located on the southern California coast, in San Diego County.
29. In a March 2019 interview, Lee Wimberley Jr. said he didn't remember much about the protests or his response to them. After college, he joined the navy.
30. The term "Texas University" is derogatorily used by critics to denote the University of Texas (Austin).
31. It is safe to assume the writer was not referring to Dean Martin, the entertainer and comedian, but actually lampooning Dean Martine by associating him with the entertainer and comedian.
32. The Haight-Ashbury district of San Francisco, California, is considered the birthplace of the 1960s counterculture movement.
33. The last line of the letter (in quotation marks) is the chorus for Bob Dylan's "Ballad of a Thin Man" from his 1965 album, *Highway 61 Revisited*.

Chapter 6

34. National Book Award winner Tim O'Brien held the endowed chair in creative writing in the Texas State English Department every other year from 1999 to 2012 and worked as a professor of creative writing, teaching several MFA workshops, in the following years.
35. The Civil Rights Act of 1964, signed into law by Texas State alumnus President Lyndon Baines Johnson on July 2, 1964, was a landmark civil rights and U.S. labor law accomplishment. It ended legal segregation in public places and banned employment discrimination on the basis of race, color, religion, sex or national origin.
36. This detail was actually reported on page fifty-one of the 1969 Texas State yearbook, the *Pedagog*.
37. *College Star*, April 12, 1968.
38. Texas Southern University is a public, historically black university located in Houston, Texas. The school was established in 1927 as the Houston Colored Junior College. In 1947, it was renamed Texas State University for Negroes. In 1951, the name changed to Texas Southern University.

39. Edwards misspoke. Thurgood Marshall never actually served as the U.S. attorney general; he served as the U.S. solicitor general from August 23, 1965, to August 30, 1967, at which time he became an associate justice of the U.S. Supreme Court and its first African American member.

40. One of Texas's two land-grant universities and the second oldest public institution of higher learning in the state, the historically black school was known as Prairie View A&M College of Texas in 1968. Today, it is known as Prairie View A&M University.

41. Dr. Alfred E. Borm sponsored the first African American club at Texas State.

42. There are several different versions (and titles) of this poem, and there is no clear, original author.

43. The John Birch Society is a far-right conservative group that supports anti-communism and limited government. "Bircherism" peaked in the 1970s, and its legacy of conspiracy theories still reverberates through conservative circles today.

44. The sum of $6 billion in 1968 is roughly the equivalent of $45 billion today.

45. In legislative procedure, a rider is an extra provision added to a bill (or other measure that is under the consideration of a legislature) that has little or no connection to the subject matter of the bill. Riders are typically inserted as a tactic to pass a controversial provision that would not pass as its own bill.

Chapter 7

46. The Higher Education Act of 1965 was reauthorized in 1968, 1972, 1976, 1980, 1986, 1992, 1998 and 2008. Current authorization for the programs in the Higher Education Act expired at the end of 2013 but was extended through 2015.

47. Scott Ritter went on to work at the *Pine Bluff Commercial*, the *Wall Street Journal* and the Dow Jones News Service, among others. He is now the production manager for *The Day* in eastern Connecticut.

48. This excerpt is from "Interview with Dan E. Farlow," which was conducted by Tylon Snodgrass in Farlow's Medina Hall office on March 11, 1986.

49. In the 1986 interview, Farlow also said the McCrocklin plagiarism issue was very damaging for Texas State and embarrassing for the educators who worked there.

50. The author of this letter unknowingly provides what was probably the McCrocklinses' exact rationale.
51. Although the two letters are signed by eleven faculty members in total, they were frequently referred to as the "Dirty Dozen." The label came from a popular film of the same name that had been released the year before.
52. Dr. Hal Brittain Pickle would go on to teach at St. Edward's University in Austin, where he remained until his passing on December 22, 1990.
53. According to a February 2019 interview with Allan Butcher, one of his students became a police officer and got to know the police officer who had informed on faculty members involved in the McCrocklin forum. At that late juncture, the informing party admitted that he had exaggerated his report and expressed shame and regret.

Chapter 8

54. The Montagnard bracelet was a symbol of friendship and respect given to U.S. Army Special Forces soldiers (Green Berets) and others during the Vietnam War. The bracelets were made of brass taken from used bullet casings.
55. William "Billy" Franklin Graham Jr. (November 7, 1918–February 21, 2018) was an American evangelist, a prominent evangelical Christian figure and an ordained Southern Baptist minister who became well known internationally in the late 1940s. According to religious historian Grant Wacker, by the mid-1960s, Graham had become the "Great Legitimator." His very presence reportedly "conferred status on presidents, acceptability on wars, shame on racial prejudice, desirability on decency, dishonor on indecency and prestige on civic events."
56. The boycott appears to have been of a local restaurant called Carson's. It had stopped serving college students after hours.
57. The sit-in was Vernon Edward's protest after Martin Luther King Jr.'s assassination.
58. Short for *argumentum ad hominem*, *ad hominem* is a fallacious argumentative strategy in which an arguing party attacks the person or persons he or she is arguing with rather than addressing the substantive points of the argument itself.
59. In a January 2019 interview, Paul Cates indicated that Robert T. Smith had had a profound influence on him. After Smith left Texas State, he began teaching at Montana State University.

60. Patricia Green Harris-Watkins passed away on August 28, 2017. When I spoke with her husband, George H. Watkins Jr., about her participation in the McCrocklin forum, he was not surprised. "She was always on the correct side of things," he said.

61. I interviewed Dr. Graham a few months before his passing on June 22, 2019. He was the J. Frank Dobie Regents Professor of American and English literature at the University of Texas and a writer-at-large for *Texas Monthly* magazine at the time. A native Texan, Graham held a PhD from the University of Texas and taught the now famous course "Life and Literature of the Southwest," first created by Dobie. He was the author of *Cowboys and Cadillacs: How Hollywood Looks at Texas* (1983); *Texas: A Literary Portrait* (1985); *No Name on the Bullet: A Biography of Audie Murphy* (1989); and *State of Minds: Texas Culture and Its Discontents* (2011).

62. The publisher of the *Hays County Free Press* and owner of the Colloquium Bookstore, Barton was a progressive force in Hays County for over fifty years until his passing on January 19, 2013. An excerpt from his obituary in the *Free Press* describes him best: "He was an unabashed liberal and lifelong Democrat who believed deeply in the promises of FDR's New Deal, JFK's idealism and LBJ's Great Society. He was a strong supporter of full participation in the political process of Hispanics, African Americans, women, students and other minorities, which often led to strong disapproval from those in the political establishment who saw him as a traitor to his roots."

63. Lawrence Welk was an American musician, bandleader and television personality who hosted the *The Lawrence Welk Show* television series from 1951 to 1982. His large audiences preferred conventional fare, and though many longtime TV shows suffered substantial ratings drops during the counterculture movement of the late 1960s, *The Lawrence Welk Show* continued to command a respectable media share.

Chapter 9

64. Denounced faculty members were in violation because they allowed students to skip class to attend the moratorium—even though the Student Senate had issued a statement supporting tolerance as well.

65. In politics, *et impera*, from Latin's *divide et impera*, means to divide and rule or divide and conquer. The concept refers to a strategy of breaking up existing large power structures into smaller, weaker power structures,

rendering them easier to rule or govern. The phrase is often attributed to Alexander the Great's father, Philip of Macedonia.

66. The protesting students' plight was brought to the attention of the ACLU by Bob Barton.

67. The dead man, who probably had his last beer with Bayless, was a twenty-five-year-old first lieutenant and forward observer named Honorio Fidel Jr. His helicopter was shot down, and it immediately burst into flames, killing everyone on board.

68. Sheldon Padgett even spoke to and managed to get quoted by the *College Star* on November 14, 1969, in its coverage of the Veteran's Day Parade (this coming after he maligned the publication the week before for presenting a "slanted, biased point of view"). "It was real inspiring," he said, "and I felt proud to be an American."

Chapter 10

69. Dr. Elmer A. DeShazo also testified at the hearing. He affirmed that his classes had been disrupted by the October demonstration.

70. Dr. Sawey was not the first faculty member to complain about other "disruptive" activities on the Quad. In a "Reader's Pulse" letter to the editor in the November 22, 1968 edition of the *College Star*, German instructor Allan Black—the same faculty member who stepped under the cordons to stand with the San Marcos 10 almost one year later—denounced the use of "outdoor public address systems, stationary or mounted on vehicles" and "pep rallies and other group activities held for the purpose of generating noise." Texas State didn't seem to have a problem with "disruptive" gatherings that it approved of.

71. George Corley Wallace Jr. (August 25, 1919–September 13, 1998) was the forty-fifth governor of Alabama. He unsuccessfully ran for president four times, and he is most remembered for his segregationist views. He opposed desegregation and supported the policies of Jim Crow during the civil rights movement, declaring in his 1963 inaugural address (as governor) that he stood for "segregation now, segregation tomorrow, segregation forever."

72. Judge Julius Jennings Hoffman (July 7, 1895–July 1, 1983) was a judge for the United States District Court for the Northern District of Illinois. He presided over the Chicago Seven trial, which was widely considered a sham. Members of the Chicago Seven (and their lawyers) were variously

found guilty, but the conviction was overturned by the U.S. Supreme Court, which ruled that Hoffman had displayed a "deprecatory and often antagonistic attitude toward the defense."

Chapter 11

73. These are the first few lines of the Vietnamese Declaration of Independence, issued on September 2, 1945: "All men are created equal; they are endowed by their Creator with certain unalienable Rights; among these are Life, Liberty, and the pursuit of Happiness." The Vietnamese quoted the American Declaration of Independence because they wanted independence. The French and the United States both attempted to deny them that.

74. Cunningham was obviously not aware of the editorial regarding the antiwar pamphlet bonfire on October 18, 1967 ("Unsure of Beliefs," *College Star*, October 20, 1967), etc.

75. See the "Peterson Report" by Dr. Norman Peterson (English Department) in the November 10, 1970 edition of the *Weather Report*. Also see "Peterson Report Revisited" by Dr. Edgar Laird (English Department) in the December 1, 1970 issue.

76. Aaron Robert "Babe" Schwartz (July 17, 1926–August 10, 2018) served in the Texas House of Representatives from 1955 to 1959 and in the Texas senate from 1960 to 1981, representing his native city of Galveston. In *Confessions of a Maddog: A Romp Through the High-Flying Texas Music and Literary Era of the Fifties to the Seventies*, Jay Dunston Milner referred to Schwartz, along with Bob Eckhardt, John Henry Faulk, Maury Maverick Jr. and others, as Texans who "fought the good fight against the Philistines" in the 1960s.

77. Today—and at that time—Rosenwasser, Satagaj, Bayless and Saranello all believe the heckler was an *agent provocateur*, who was possibly brought in from outside the university.

78. Joe R. Lansdale has written forty-six novels and published thirty short story collections in several genres, including western, horror, science fiction, mystery and suspense. He has received numerous awards for his writing, and his works have been adapted into a number of films (*Bubba Ho-Tep*, 2002; *Christmas with the Dead*, 2012; *Cold in July*, 2014; etc.) and television series (*Hap and Leonard*, 2016–18).

Chapter 12

79. The Student Nonviolent Coordinating Committee, or SNCC (often pronounced /snɪk/ SNIK), was a major American civil rights movement organization in the early 1960s. It emerged from the first wave of student civil rights sit-ins and formed at a May 1960 meeting organized by Ella Baker at Shaw University. After its involvement in the Voter Education Project, SNCC grew into a pivotal civil rights organization with many supporters in the North and South, allowing full-time organizers to have a small salary. Many volunteer grassroots organizers and activists also worked with SNCC on projects in the Deep South, often becoming targets of racial violence and police brutality. SNCC played an important role in the freedom rides, the 1963 March on Washington, Mississippi Freedom Summer, the Selma campaigns, the March Against Fear and other civil rights events.

80. Elizabeth Crook is the award-winning author of several books, including *The Raven's Bride* (1991), *Promised Lands* (1994), *The Night Journal* (2006), *Monday, Monday* (2014) and *The Which Way Tree* (2018).

81. Held every May 5, Cinco de Mayo commemorates the Mexican Army's victory over the French empire at the Battle of Puebla on May 5, 1862, under the leadership of General Ignacio Zaragoza. Zaragoza was born in modern-day Goliad, Texas.

82. As dedicated and protective as the community of San Marcos was in terms of LBJ's war during that era, the town seems to have been entirely ignorant of his 1968 Bilingual Education Act, which was the first piece of federal legislation that recognized the needs of Limited English Speaking Ability (LESA) students.

Chapter 13

83. The first time I wrote about the San Marcos 10 was in the spring 1989 issue of the Texas State student magazine, *Hillside Scene*. Members of the group actually invited me to attend the reunion, but unfortunately, I was otherwise preoccupied.

84. Dr. Randall Bland witnessed the San Marcos 10 protest from his second-floor classroom window. "The disruption was caused by the onlookers," Bland told the *Hillside Scene* magazine in 1989. "Especially the rodeo association and the athletic fraternity."

85. The sum of $100,000 in 1981 is roughly the equivalent of $270,000 in 2019.
86. Palomo is unfortunately unable to remember his formerly conservative cowboy friend's name.
87. David Bayless had left Texas State to join the military in late 1965. The fall semester of 1969 was his first semester back.

Chapter 14

88. The Vietnamese refer to the Vietnam War as "America's War." The Gulf of Tonkin incident(s) used to initiate the conflict were not provocations—they were pure prevarications. The engagement was unprovoked, and the Vietnamese nomenclature for the conflict is correct.
89. The 1962 Port Huron Statement is a political manifesto of the American student activist movement Students for a Democratic Society (SDS).
90. The Seattle Seven were the most prominent members of the Seattle Liberation Front, an antiwar organization formed in Seattle just as SDS was dissolving.

BIBLIOGRAPHY

Abilene Reporter-News. "Ft. Hood Negro Soldiers Refuse to Go to Chicago." August 25, 1968.

———. "Protest Bid Support Fails." May 22, 1969.

———. "'San Marcos 10' Back in College." December 14, 1969.

———. "'San Marcos 10' Ruling Expected." November 29, 1969.

———. "10 Students Ousted for M-Day Protest." November 14, 1969.

———. "Viet Protest Opens with Vigils, Rallies." November 14, 1969.

Albrecht, Jan. "Anti-war Leaflets Stir Emotions." *College Star*, October 20, 1967.

Albuquerque Journal. "10 Students' Suspension Upheld." November 25, 1969.

Austin American-Statesman. "ACLU Files Suit for Damages in Suspensions at San Marcos." November 21, 1969.

———. "Court Says Teacher Gets SWT Post." February 26, 1981.

———. "Court Upholds Protest Ruling." May 16, 1972.

———. "8 Return to SWT After Court Ruling." December 16, 1969.

———. "Justice—At Last." November 1, 1981.

———. "McCrocklin Defends Paper." February 25, 1969.

———. "McCrocklin Is Defrocked." November 1, 1969.

———. "McCrocklin Quits SWT's Presidency." April 20, 1969.

———. "Protests Over U.S. Focus on War Dead." November 15, 1969.

———. "Rule Upholds Student Right." February 25, 1969.

———. "San Marcos, SWT Pupils Join in Vets Day Fetes." November 1, 1969.

———. "Students Plan Sit-In at SWT." February 20, 1969.

——. "SWT Professor Calls Re-Election." January 8, 1969.

———. "10 Receive Suspension at SWT." November 14, 1969.

———. "10 Students Denied Credits to Appeal to Higher Court." January 12, 1971.

———. "UT Mounts 'Study' of Disputed Paper." February 25, 1969.

Banta, Bob, and Jerri Martin. "SWT Professor Wins Reinstatement Ruling." *Austin American-Statesman*, October 1980.

Big Spring Daily Herald. "'San Marcos 10' Lawyer Will Appeal." January 12, 1971.

Blackmon, Steve. "Hecklers Boo Hippies, Hippies Return 'Favor.'" *College Star*, October 17, 1969.

———. "Newspaper Defined by Editor." *College Star*, November 14, 1969.

———. "Resolution Charges Impugned by *Star*." *College Star*, November 7, 1969.

Brinkley, Douglas, and Luke A. Nichter. *The Nixon Tapes, 1971–1972*. Boston: Mariner Books, 2015.

Broad, William, and Nicolas Wade. *Betrayers of the Truth: Fraud and Deceit in the Halls of Science*. New York: Simon and Schuster, 1982.

Brown, Ronald C., and David C. Nelson. *Up the Hill, Down the Years: A Century in the Life of the College in San Marcos*. Virginia Beach: Donning Publishers, 1999.

Brownwood Bulletin. "Dec. 4 Decision Due on Students." November 30, 1969.

———. "SWT Cool to Protests." October 20, 1967.

———. "Ten STS Students Win Readmission." December 14, 1969.

———. "10 Students Lose Appeal." November 25, 1969.

Burrell, Katie. "The San Marcos 10 Talk Protests." *University Star*, May 19, 2017.

Cherokeean, The. "Moratorium Post Mortems." November 15, 1969.

College Star. "Academic Freedom Queried." April 4, 1969.

———. "Anti-war Protests Draw UT Students." October 27, 1967.

———. "Articles Draw Fire; Poems Latest Fad." October 31, 1969.

———. "Campus to Be the Site of Rally in Protest of Vietnam War." October 10, 1969.

———. "Cartoon Choice, Rules Subject of Concern." December 5, 1969.

———. "Differing Opinions Cover It All." November 24, 1968.

———. "Dissenters' Efforts in Vain?" December 12, 1969.

———. "Garrett Resigns Senate Position Monday Night." December 5, 1969.

———. "Hill Removes Anti-Vietnam Art." August 18, 1969.

———. "Hippies Can Help Us, Too." February 21, 1969.

———. "It Is Our War!" May 6, 1966.

————. "King's Death Draws Comment." April 12, 1968.

————. "LBJ Visit Surprises SWT." January 31, 1969.

————. "Letters Complain, Urge." November 1, 1968.

————. "Majority Votes Demonstrations Not Disturbing." November 21, 1969.

————. "March On!" April 12, 1968.

————. "March to Honor Flag, War Dead." November 7, 1969.

————. "McCrocklin Chosen HEW Undersecretary." June 14, 1968.

————. "McCrocklin Confirmed." October 4, 1968.

————. "McCrocklin Work in CIA." April 14, 1967.

————. "Moratoriums Should Continue." October 17, 1969.

————. "New President Assumes Duties Sept. 1, Jones 'Looks to the Future' of SWTSU." August 15, 1969.

————. "Open Resistance Predicted." October 27, 1967.

————. "Prexy Speaks Out." February 28, 1969.

————. "Principles of Criticism, Free Opinion Supported." November 7, 1969.

————. "Profs Hit McCrocklin Defense." December 15, 1968.

————. "Protesters' Vigil Set Tuesday." December 12, 1969.

————. "Regents Nullify PhD." November 7, 1969.

————. "Riots for Peace?" April 12, 1968.

————. "Sad Day in Mudville." November 14, 1969.

————. "Senate Asks *Star* Review." November 7, 1969.

————. "Senate, Professor Draw Comments; Alumnus, Student Defend 'Star.'" November 14, 1969.

————. "Senate Sets Wednesday Referendum to Gauge Opinions of Moratoriums." November 14, 1969.

————. "'Silent Majority' Lashes Out." November 21, 1969.

————. "*Star* Not Censored." October 27, 1967.

————. "*Star* Presents 'Uncensored' Paper; Administration Statement Questioned." December 12, 1969.

————. "Student Dismissal, 'New Generation' Topics of Reader Interest." November 14, 1969.

————. "Student Protesters Denied Financial Aid." September 20, 1968.

————. "Student Protestors Suspended at Unauthorized Rally Thursday." November 14, 1969.

————. "Students Air View on Moratorium." October 17, 1969.

————. "Students Disagree with Moratorium, Senate, Administration." November 21, 1969.

————. "Students Protest Prof Removal." June 13, 1969.

————. "Students Still Question Demonstration." October 24, 1969.

———. "Tell It Like It Is." September 27, 1968.

———. "Truth Is…" October 27, 1967.

———. "Unsigned Letter Draws Reply." January 31, 1969.

———. "Unsure of Beliefs?" October 20, 1967.

———. "War Stand Draws Comment." April 12, 1968.

———. "Writers Protest, Defend Protesters." October 27, 1967.

———. "Writers Reply to Statement." February 28, 1969.

Collier, Terry. "McCrocklin Gives Reply to Doubters." *College Star*, February 28, 1969.

———. "McCrocklin Paper Reviewed." *College Star*, September 27, 1968.

———. "Small Group Mourns Martin L. King." *College Star*, April 12, 1968.

Cook, John. "Roger Ailes' Secret Nixon-Era Blueprint for Fox News." *Gawker*, June 30, 2011.

Corsicana Daily Sun. "Federal Court Balks Student Suspensions." November 13, 1969.

———. "Suspended Students Are Planning Fight." November 25, 1969.

Cowder, Ruth Ann. "Moratorium Resolution Fails." *College Star*, October 17, 1969.

———. "Senate Again Considers Further McCrocklin Stand." *College Star*, March 7, 1969.

Cunningham, Bill. "The Death of a Student Newspaper." *Purgatory Creek Press*, January 6, 1970.

———. "President Resigns, Bitterly Blasts Foes." *College Star*, April 25, 1969.

———. "Protesters Brave Drizzle." *College Star*, February 21, 1969.

———. "Senate Acknowledges Defense of Dissertation." *College Star*, February 28, 1969.

———. "Students Protest War in Local Moratorium." *College Star*, October 17, 1969.

Daily Record. "Protesters Still Carry Torch for Free Speech." October 24, 2001.

Dallas Morning News. "Court Act Reinstates 10 Suspended Students at SWTSU." December 14, 1969.

———. "Students Protest in San Marcos." December 18, 1969.

———. "Suspensions at SWTSU Protested by Students." November 15, 1969.

DeBenedetti, Charles, and Charles Chatfield. *An American Ordeal: The Antiwar Movement of the Vietnam Era*. Syracuse, NY: Syracuse University Press, 1990.

Denman, Bob. "Instructor, Student Leader Hit McCrocklin Statement." *Austin American-Statesman*, February 26, 1969.

Denton Record-Chronicle. "Goldfish Starts Trouble." April 10, 1975.

Dugger, Ronnie. "Sex and the College President." *Texas Observer*, April 28, 1967.

El Paso Times. "Kick Out Students at Peace Rally." November 14, 1969.

———. "U.S. Delegates Minimize Support for Moratorium." November 14, 1969.

Evans, Derro. "UT Mounts 'Study' of Disputed Paper." *Austin American-Statesman*, February 25, 1969.

Ford, Jon. "McCrocklin Brings Dynamism to SWTSC." *San Antonio Express*, January 9, 1965.

Galveston Daily News. "25 Stage Protest at STSU." December 18, 1969.

Gardner, Fred. "The Fort Hood 43." *Counterpunch*, January 31, 2017.

Goodbread, Stephany S. "Interview with Dr. Richard B. Henderson." University Archives, Texas State University. October 17, 1985.

Hanson, Chuck. "Controversy Continues as Statement Fans Fire." *College Star*, February 28, 1969.

Harper Herald. "An Erosion of Spirit." October 31, 1969.

Haster, Linda. "Board of Regents Uphold Ruling, Lawyers File Suit for Damages." *College Star*, December 5, 1969.

———. "Review Board Finds Protesters Guilty." *College Star*, November 21, 1969

Henry, John C. "SWT Asks Court to Cancel Reinstatement." *Austin American-Statesman*, January 3, 1981.

Houston Post. "School Boots 10 Following Rally." November 14, 1969.

Howard, Jane. "Freedom Not Free, Past Shows Cost." *College Star*, November 21, 1969.

Howze, Sara. "Expelled 10 Sue SWT for Credit." *Austin American-Statesman*, January 9. 1971.

Hughes, Candace. "Court Says Teacher Gets SWT Post." *Austin American-Statesman*, February 26, 1981.

Kennedy, Ira. "Peace Movement." *Weather Report*, November 10, 1970.

King, Carol Seminar. "Martine Resigns Amid Funds Controversy." *University Star*, May 2, 1975.

Kissinger, Henry A. *White House Years*. Boston: Little, Brown and Company, 1979.

Laird, Edgar S. "Peterson Report Revisited: Matter of Style." *Weather Report*, December 1, 1970.

Longview News-Journal. "Fired Professor Ordered Reinstated." October 29, 1980.

———. "Southwest Texas State Students' Appeal Fails." May 19, 1972.

Lubbock Avalanche-Journal. "Few Show for 'Study-In.'" May 22, 1969.

Luther, Shae R. "The McCrocklin Affair: Academic Integrity and Presidential Plagiarism at Southwest Texas State College." Master's thesis, Texas State University, May 2008.

Marshall News Messenger. "Moratorium Planners Eye November." October 16, 1969.

Martin, Jerri. "Hays Grand Jury Eyes SWT Funds Incident." *Austin American-Statesman*, June 5, 1975.

———. "Judge Delays Student Ruling." *Austin American-Statesman*, November 29, 1969.

———. "San Marcos, SWT Pupils Join in Vets Day Parade." *Austin American-Statesman*, November 12, 1969.

———. "Students Hit Ouster at SWT." *Austin American-Statesman*, November 15, 1969.

———. "SWT's Suspension of Students Upheld." *Austin American-Statesman*, November 19, 1969.

Mexia Daily News. "Ten Students Suspended for Demonstration." November 16, 1969.

Murdoch, Pat. "10 Students Suspended." *Southwest Texas State University Press Release*, November 13, 1969.

Northcott, Kaye. "A Forum on McCrocklin." *Texas Observer*, December 27, 1968.

Odessa American. "Long-Hairs Win Case in College Test." October 5, 1972.

———. "'San Marcos 10' Gets Readmittance Hearing." December 14, 1969.

———. "SWTSU Students Won't Get Supreme Court Hearing." May 16, 1972.

Oldham, Lydia, and Henrietta Turk. "Statement Adequate?" *College Star*, February 28, 1969.

Olds, Greg. "The AAUP Awaiting Further Developments at Odessa, SWT." *Texas Observer*, June 6, 1969.

———. "The McCrocklin Dissertation." *Texas Observer*, August 9, 1968.

Palomo, Juan Ramon. "How It Started." *Weather Report*, November 10, 1970.

Pedagog. "Demonstrators Mourn King Death, Protest Campus 'Prejudice.'" 1968

Peterson, Norman. "The Peterson Report." *Weather Report*, November 10, 1970.

Pfeffer, John. "One in a Line." *Weather Report*, December 1, 1970.

———. "University Star." *Weather Report*, November 10, 1970.

Purgatory Creek Press. "Fight Prof. Ouster." February 22, 1970.

———. "Moratorium Makes It." January 6, 1970.

———. "San Marcos 10." February 22, 1970.

———. "San Marcos 10 Lose to Kangaroos." December 9, 1969.

Reiner, Bernard. "Book Review." *History of Education Quarterly*, Spring 1968.

Rhines, Barbara. "Senate Defeats 'Severity' Idea." *College Star*, November 21, 1969.

Ritter, Scott. "McCrocklin's Defrocking." *Hillside Scene*, Spring 1990.

Rodriguez, Erik. "The Power of Protest." *Austin American-Statesman*, October 24, 2001.

San Antonio Express. "Group at SWT Plans 'Study-In.'" May 21, 1969.

———. "His Complete Statement." February 25, 1969.

———. "McCrocklin Cleared by Board." August 21, 1968.

———. "San Marcos Moratorium Held Without Incidents." October 16, 1969.

———. "SWT Student Dean Resigns." April 30, 1975.

San Antonio Light. "Board Denies Appeal of Students." November 25, 1969.

———. "10 Protesting Students Expelled at Southwest." November 14, 1969.

San Marcos Mercury. "'San Marcos 10' to Relive Protesting the Vietnam War." May 10, 2017.

Snodgrass. Tylon. "Interview with Daniel E. Farlow." March 11, 1986.

Stevens, Ann. "Senate Backs Administration." *College Star*, November 21, 1969.

Sullivan, Gerald, and Zaroulis, Nancy. *Who Spoke Up? American Protest Against the War in Vietnam 1963–1975*. New York: Holt, Rinehart and Winston, 1984.

Thiele, Nick. "Student Questions Denial." *College Star*, November 8, 1968.

University Star. "Student Rights Often Stifled." December 3, 1971.

———. "Through the Years: University Protection of Free Speech Expands Over the Decades." February 18, 2015.

Veidt, Jerri. "Protests Peaceful at SWT." *Austin American-Statesman*, February 21, 1969.

———. "SWT Rejects UT Peacenicks." *Austin American-Statesman*, October 20, 1967.

———. "SWT 'Study-In' Attracts Only 50." *Austin American-Statesman*, May 22, 1969.

Wells, Tom. *The War Within: America's Battle Over Vietnam*. Berkeley: University of California Press, 1994.

Zaroulis, Nancy, and Gerald Sullivan. *Who Spoke Up? American Protest Against the War in Vietnam 1963–1975*. New York: Holt, Rinehart and Winston, 1984.

INDEX

A

academic freedom 37, 46–47, 50, 52, 103, 108
ACLU 52, 109, 119, 121, 126, 155, 166, 179, 184
Adams, John Quincy 81–82, 149, 154
African American 69, 77, 81, 152, 153, 181
Agnew, Spiro 26
Ailes, Roger 173–176
Albrecht, Jan 65
American Association of University Professors 97
American Political Science Association 101
"America the Beautiful" 142
Aransas Pass, TX 18
Archer, Ben 92
Arlington National Cemetery 16
assassination 69, 72, 87, 164, 166, 171, 178, 182

Associated Student Government, Texas State University 29, 127, 159
Association of Women Students (AWS) 158
Austin American-Statesman 55, 121, 154–155, 158, 162, 189
Austin Chronicle 95
Austin Public Library 170

B

baby boomers 176
Bagley, Thomas R. 118
Barton, Bob 32, 101–102, 151, 184
Barton, Weldon V. 49
Basye, David 123
Bayless, David 18, 39, 56, 95, 114, 116, 139–142, 150, 157, 170, 171, 184, 185
Bednar, Bill 159
Being Nixon: A Man Divided 109

Berkman, Cliff 55, 57–58, 63–64, 165

Betrayers of Truth: Fraud and Deceit in the Halls of Science 100

Big Lebowski, The 15, 170

Bilingual Education Act, 1968 186

Billboard Hot 100 15

Black, Allan 18, 113, 184

Blackmon, Steve 37, 108, 118, 123, 127, 136–137, 139

Black Panthers 139

Bland, Randall 161

Blue Cross Blue Shield Student Health Plan 160

Board of Regents, Texas State University System 84, 86, 96, 104, 107, 121, 124, 138, 149, 155, 161, 162

Borm, Alfred E. 70, 181

Bourne, Randolph 34

Bowman, Dave 107

Brooklyn, NY 18

Brookshier, Kyle C. 36

Brunson, Martha Luan 149

Bryson, James R. 36

Buckley, Frank 136–139

Buckner, Addison 138

Building Citizenship 82

Burleson, Annie 18, 110–111, 114, 120, 121, 122, 157, 170–171

Bush, George H.W. 176

Bush, George W. 173

Butcher, Allan 90, 97–98, 101, 149, 182

C

Cambodia 143

Cambodian Campaign 24

Campus Christian Community (CCC) 29, 32

Camus, Albert 5

Canyon High School 60

Cates, Paul 18, 19, 25, 97, 103, 112–114, 119–120, 140, 170, 182

Cedar Chopper's Almanack 83

Champagne, Gerald 161

Chandler, Charles 81–83, 149, 154

Chatfield, John 118

Cheney, Dick 175–176

Chernikowski, Stephanie 70

Chicago 67, 72–73, 77, 132, 189

Christian 156

CIA 20, 24, 36, 79, 156

civil disobedience 168

civil rights 40, 42, 66, 71–72, 152, 175

Clift, Paula Gene 126

Cofer, Hume 162

College Star 29–30, 33–34, 39, 42, 46–47, 51, 55, 56, 58, 63, 71, 84–90, 95, 98, 105, 107, 114, 118, 121, 122, 127, 130, 136, 148, 155, 164, 184–185

Collier, Terry 85

Colloquium Bookstore 102

Communists 24, 36, 57, 76

Communist sympathizers 23

Connally, John 79

Constitution 121, 132

Corb, Alvin 33

Corbin, Pat 131

Corrie, Walter 161

Country Music, USA 47
Crawford Ranch 173
Crockett State School 42
Crook, Elizabeth 153, 186
Crook, William 150, 152
Cunningham, Bill 30, 130, 135, 136, 154–155, 169

D

Daily Texan 45, 85
Democratic National Convention 77
Denton Public Library 102
Derrick, Leland 92, 100, 118
DeShazo, Elmer A. 184
Detroit News 85, 92
Dibrell, Steve 103
"Dirty Dozen" 182
Dorn, William Jennings Bryan 110
Douglas, William 146
Dylan, Bob 31, 178, 180

E

Edwards, Vernon 68–70, 72–73, 164, 182
Elliott, James D. 118
Ellis, Nancy Hanks 126, 154, 168
Ellis, Peter F. 34
Ellsberg, Daniel 169
El Paso, TX 20, 44
Emancipation Park 40
Emory, William A. 90–91
Ermis, Ellen 114
Etheridge, Eddy 46, 154–155, 169

F

Fall, Bernard 49
Farlow, Daniel E. 29, 38, 81, 84, 90, 94
fascist 103
Fifth U.S. Circuit Court of Appeals 132, 144, 146
First Amendment 64, 109, 119, 120, 121, 126, 132, 156, 165, 167, 171
Flores, Geronimo "Jerry" 154
Fly, William 162
Fort Hood 22, 37, 48, 50, 77
Fort Hood 43 77
Fort Hood Three 22, 48, 50
Fort Worth 102
Fowler, Severra 153
Fowler, William "Bill" 148–150, 153–155, 167
Fox News 174, 175
freedom of the press 136
free speech 17, 50, 52, 60, 63, 87, 109, 119, 122, 156, 158, 168
Fresno Bee 39
"Friends of Floyd Martine" 162

G

Garrett, Kent 29, 37, 111–112, 114, 127, 130, 132, 138
Gates, Amos 42
Gatesville School for Boys 42
gender discrimination 159
Geneva Accords of 1964 65
"geographic diversity" 149
Giap, Vo Nguyen 135
Gielow, Charles 31, 106

Gier, Bob 88
Goliad, TX 115
Goodbread, Stephany S. 166
Goodell, Charles E. 110
Gorden, William I. 50–54, 141
Graham, Billy 95
Graham, Don 98, 101
Grayson, Nancy 149
Green, Don Caroll 118
Green, James 97
Grimm, Clyde 148, 167
guerrilla warfare 50
Gulf of Tonkin Resolution 86

H

Hahn, Cecil 42
Haldeman, H.R. 23
Hanoi apologists 23
Hanson, Chuck 58
Hap and Leonard, book and TV
    series 147, 185
Harden, Paul 144, 146
Harmon, Gordon 150, 152, 153
Harris, Patricia Green 90, 101,
    183
Hart, Franklin A. 85
"Hart Report" 85
Haster, Linda 138
Hays County Citizen 42, 83
Hays County Free Press 32, 151
Hays County, TX 81–82, 161
Hazard, Mary 130
Heinl, R.D. 85, 92, 94
Henderson, Richard B. 62, 123,
    166
Henderson, Richard B., Jr. 62
Hendrix, Jimi 95

Henson, Al 18, 53, 110–112, 119,
    132, 164, 170, 171
Higher Education Act 79, 181
Hill Hints 116, 121
Hill, John 159
Hillside Scene 28, 79, 80, 92, 104,
    186
Hinojosa, Jose 29, 31, 38
Hinton, Billy J. 54
hippies 32–33, 95, 96, 103, 113,
    114
History of Education Quarterly 82
Hitler, Adolph 107
Hobbs, James B. 69, 111, 119, 141
Ho Chi Minh 76
Hoffman, Julius 132
Holloway, Barron 55, 57, 63, 64
Holman, Brooks 119
Holman, Michael 18, 53, 142, 145,
    170, 171
Houston, Ralph H. 105, 148
Howard, Jane 130, 137–138
Howe, Henry H., Jr. 44
Hughes, Ray Osgood 82
Huntsville Action for Youth (HA-
    YOU) 39
Huntsville, TX 39–40, 42, 43, 149
Hurd, John A., Jr. 52
Hutchinson, L.H. 144, 146

I

Institute of Race Relations 101
Iraq War 173

J

Jackson State University 144
Jackson, Wendell 129
Jarrett, Bobby 69
Johnson, James, Jr. 48
Johnson, Lyndon Baines (LBJ) 21, 148, 180
"Johnson restriction" 54
Jones, Billy Mac 111, 126
Jones, Chuck 130
Jordan, Mel 90

K

kangaroo court 132
Keck, Ted 161
Kennedy High School, San Antonio, TX 170
Kennedy, John F. 171
Kenny Rogers and the New Edition 15
Kent, OH 25 141
Kent State University 53, 141–143, 173
Kiker, Mary Alice 36, 179
Killeen, TX 77
King, Martin Luther, Jr. (MLK) 40, 66, 71, 178
Kingsville, TX 78–79, 83
Kinsey report 52
Kissinger, Henry 23
KKK 40
Komondosky, Edmond S. 74
Korean War 21, 30
Kreiner, George 50, 179

L

Lamar University 19
Lansdale, Joe R. 144, 146, 147, 185
La Otra Voz 153
Lawson, Bill 40
Levbarg, Mark 119, 126, 166
Liberal Party 43
Ligarde, Sherry 114
Lincoln, Abraham 57
Lockhart, TX 18
London, England 101
London, Jack 125
Longoria, Ralph 133
Lupu, Sidney 31, 37, 163, 179
Luther, Shae R. 83

M

Maddox, Bill 119, 141
Maddox, Luise 126
Making of the Modern World, The 78
Malik, Y.K. 101
Malone, Bill C. 39–43, 45–47, 154–155
March Against Death 16
"Marine's Vietnam Diary" 50, 179
Marshall, Steve 90, 101
Marshall, Thurgood 70, 181
Martin, Dean 60
Martine, Floyd 17, 31, 55–56, 64, 69–70, 72, 79, 87, 88, 97, 103, 109, 111, 113–114, 125, 132, 141, 157, 158, 162
Massey, David 54–55, 63–64
McCabe, Terry 114, 178
McCarthy, Joseph 107

McConchie, David O. 18, 114, 132, 170
McConnell, James 142
"McCrocklin flu" 103, 165
McCrocklin, James H. 39, 42, 45, 78–104, 107, 124
Memphis State University 149
Mendez, Celestino 153
Metcalf, Clyde H. 85
Mexican American 81, 152–154
Mexican American Youth Organization (MAYO) 153
military-industrial complex 66
Miller, Bill 107
Milner, Jay Dunston 185
Mora, Dennis 48
Moreno, Tonia Gayle 159
Morris, Roger 24
Morse, Wayne 86
Murdock, Pat 18
Murray State University 47
My Lai Massacre 16, 22

N

NAACP 81
napalm 145
National Advisory Committee on Selective Service 79
New Braunfels, TX 51
Newman Club 31, 178
New Mobilization Committee to End the War in Vietnam (New Mobe) 16
New York City 66, 73, 101
New York Times 68
1970s 155, 158, 175, 185
1960s 15, 176

Nixon administration 24–25, 110, 175
Nixon, Richard 21, 75, 110, 141
North Vietnam 25, 35, 73, 110

O

Oakes, Wayne 40, 155, 179
O'Brien, Tim 66
October Surprise 25
Odell, John S. 98
Ohio National Guard 141
Oldham, Lydia 98
101st Airborne 56
Owens, Mike 141, 142

P

Padgett, Sheldon 123
Palomo, Juan R. 28, 78, 105, 114, 152, 155, 165
panty raid 142
Pasadena, TX 18
Peaceniks 55, 57, 165
Pentagon Papers 169
People's History of the United States, The 168
Pfeffer, John 30, 87, 97, 139, 149
Pickle, Hal B. 90
Pickle, J.J. 155
Pinkerton, Frank 40
"pinko" 57, 62
Pisk, George 148
plagiarism 83–84, 86, 88, 91, 92, 93, 94, 100, 123, 166, 181
Pool, William C. 29, 38, 126
Port Huron Statement 187

Preibisch, Billy 168
Price, Ray 23
Pullen, C.H.W. 82
Purgatory Creek Press (PCP) 130–136, 139

Q

Quanstrom, Kathy 74

R

Randolph Air Force Base 64, 75
Ravelo, Adam C. 18
"Reader's Pulse" 34, 44, 56, 58, 72, 87–89, 98, 105, 107, 123, 127, 129, 184
Reagan, Ronald 39, 176, 178
Red China 75
Reed, Pamela 44
Rexall Cowpersons 62
Rhodes Middle School, San Antonio, TX 170
Rice, Grantland 113
Rice University 20
Rietz, Roger 105
Ritter, Scott 11, 80, 181
Roberts, Jack 132, 146, 149
Robertson, Rob 46
Robinson, Jerry 95
Roche, Bruce 51
Rodeo Cowboys' Association, Texas State 126
Rohingya 171
Rolling Stone 173
Roosevelt, Theodore 78

Rosenwasser, Murray 18, 56, 97, 114–115, 139–142, 170, 185
Rubin, Jerry 15
Ruiz, Ruben 152–153
Rumsfeld, Donald 175

S

Saenz, Gilbert Ortiz 153
Safire, William 110
Samas, David A. 48
Sam Houston High School 40, 42
Sam Houston State University 40, 149
Sampson, Alfred A. 40
San Antonio Light 23
San Marcos Consolidated Independent School District (SMCISD) 150, 152, 155, 168
San Marcos Record 138
Saranello, Joe 18, 28, 29, 38, 61, 114–115, 121, 140–143, 146, 170–171
Satagaj, Sallie Ann 18, 30, 36, 56, 97, 103, 114, 158, 170, 171, 173
Sawey, Ronald M. 129
Schatzki, George 52
Schneider v. New Jersey 126
Schulze, Glenn 60
Schwartz, A.R. "Babe" 140
Sealy, TX 18, 168
Seattle Seven 170
Sensing, Thurman 110
Shirer, William L. 156
silent majority 110, 122
Sims, Charles 159

Sisto, Tony 111, 114
Smisek, Pam 137–139
Smith, Lee H. 160, 162
Smith, Robert T. 90, 182
Southern Christian Leadership Conference 40
Southern Methodist University 19
Soviet Union 75
Sparkman, Porter 51–54, 135, 179
Spencer, Jerry 64, 75
Stalin, Joseph 107
"Star-Spangled Banner, The" 72
Statue of Liberty 72
Student-Faculty Review Board 112, 118, 121, 126, 131
Student Mobilization Committee 16
Students' Committee for Professors' Rights 46
Student Senate, Texas State University 30, 97, 107, 110, 119, 121, 123, 127, 128, 130, 137, 183
"Study of the Garde d'Haiti, A" 82
Sullivan, Gerald 26
Sullivan, John 21
Sulsar, Lois P. 126
Svec, Marilyn 114

T

Tarleton State University 20
Texas Association of College Teachers 79
Texas Monthly 151
Texas Municipal League 79
Texas Observer 21, 51, 54, 84, 85, 184

Texas State University News Service 116, 123
Texas Supreme Court 162
Texas Tech University 82
Thiele, Nick 73, 74, 87, 88
Things They Carried, The 66
Thomas, Evan 109
Thomas, William 29
Thompson, Hunter S. 173
Thurmond, Strom 110
Tiananmen Square 171
Time Magazine 85
Tinker v. Des Moines Community School District 126
Travis County, TX 126
Trump, Donald J. 176
Tulane University 47
Tumbleson, Daryl W. 56, 62–64
Turner, Nat 70
"TV war" 175
Tyler Junior College 144, 146

U

UNESCO 86
University of Texas 19, 40, 45, 47, 52, 55, 79, 97–101, 104, 149
University of Texas at El Paso 20
University Star 39, 135, 139, 145, 159
U.S. Department of Health, Education and Welfare 79, 92
U.S. Senate Foreign Relations Committee 86

V

Vietnam Moratorium Committee
16
Voltaire 105
Vykoukal, Frances 18, 29, 30, 61,
114, 118, 119, 120, 168

Z

Zaroulis, Nancy 26
Zinn, Howard 168

W

Walker, Bill 138
"War Is the Health of the State" 34
Washington, D.C. 16, 73, 85, 96,
140
Washington Post 68, 86
Watergate scandal 173
Waters, Phil 153
Weather Report 139, 149, 185
Wenz, Udo 152
Whitehead, Tom 25
*Who Spoke Up? American Protest Against
the War in Vietnam 1963–1975*
26
Wilson, Joe H. 92
Wilson, Thomas 54
Wimberley, Lee, Jr. 30, 58
Wimberley, TX 111
Winsett, Walter A. 29, 38, 90, 102
Wisconsin, University of 47

Y

Young Republicans Club 30, 58

ABOUT THE AUTHOR

E.R. BILLS GRADUATED FROM Texas State University with a degree in journalism in 1990. He is the author of *Texas Obscurities: Stories of the Peculiar, Exceptional and Nefarious* (The History Press, 2013), *The 1910 Slocum Massacre: An Act of Genocide in East Texas* (The History Press, 2014), *Black Holocaust: The Paris Horror and a Legacy of Texas Terror* (Eakin Press, 2015) and *Texas Far & Wide: The Tornado with Eyes, Gettysburg's Last Casualty, The Celestial Skipping Stone and Other Tales* (The History Press, 2017). Bills has also written for publications around the state, including *Texas Co-Op Power* magazine, *Fort Worth Weekly*, *Fort Worth, TX* magazine, the *Fort Worth Star-Telegram* and the *Austin-American Statesman*. He currently lives in north Texas with his wife, Stacie.

Visit us at
www.historypress.com
···